CHRIST'S O

'To him who is able to k. _ _.. jr um stumbling' shouts of
the activity of Christ's life, death, resurrection, ascension and
continuing intercession for us. We are sustained by Christ
from moment to moment, just as he sustained the lives of
those who nailed him to the cross. There is nothing passive in
the work of Christ: David Gay ably demonstrates this from
Scripture.

Steve Guest

Whenever David Gay writes on any theological topic, I know
it will be well worth reading – all the more so on such a
precious doctrine as the imputation of Christ's obedience to
believers! Furthermore, it is an important time for David to
publish this work, seeing as some within NCT (new-covenant
theology) circles (and beyond) are now denying the doctrine
of the imputed (active) obedience of Christ and openly
teaching against it. With David, I am convinced that Scripture
does teach the doctrine, and that, rather than being
inconsistent with NCT, it is necessitated by it, seeing as the
old covenant had to be fulfilled by Christ so that he could
establish a new covenant with believers who are in union with
him, and his righteousness that fulfilled the law. I regard this
to be a doctrine of great importance and of, perhaps,
unrivalled comfort for believers. I am delighted, therefore,
that David has published this book, and I pray that it will
have a great impact. I have personally profited from reading
David's various articles on the subject that are now brought
together in this work and I heartily commend them to all.

George Platt

David Gay gives gave a clear, plain and biblical explanation
about justification of sinners in God's sight. It is grounded on
Christ's complete and perfect obedience (Rom. 5:19) to the
Father's law (Rom. 8:3-4, Matt. 5:17) and will (John 4:34).
This perfect obedience is done **wilfully** and **actively** until he
uttered the last words: 'It is finished!' I heartily agree that
justification is not forgiveness alone, but includes imputation
of God's or Christ's righteousness to believers. Yes,
justification is through faith in Christ.

Percival Tanierla

Books by David H.J.Gay referred to in this volume:

Amyraut & Owen Tested and Found Wanting.

Assurance in the New Covenant.

Baptist Sacramentalism: A Warning to Baptists.

Believers Under the Law of Christ.

Christ is All: No Sanctification by the Law.

Fivefold Sanctification.

Four 'Antinomians' Tried and Vindicated.

Infant Baptism Tested.

Peter Masters' Muddle over the Covenants.

Positional Sanctification: Two Consequences.

Redemption History Through Covenants.

Romans 11: A Suggested Exegesis.

Sanctification in Galatians.

Sanctification in Jeremiah.

Sanctification in Philippians.

Sanctification in Romans.

The Hinge in Romans 1 – 8: A critique of N.T.Wright's view of Baptism and Conversion.

The New Covenant in Ezekiel: An Introduction.

Christ's Obedience Imputed

David H.J.Gay

BRACHUS

BRACHUS 2018
davidhjgay@googlemail.com

Contents

Introduction

Since 'the imputed righteousness of Christ' is still a matter of warm debate in some circles, I have produced this book by taking my articles on the subject, editing them only very lightly while leaving them in their chronological order of original publication. This will make it easier for those who want to have my views on the question, and it will also make the material more permanent.

'Imputed righteousness'? While the phrase does not appear in Scripture, almost all believers use it. In any case, as long as we bear in mind that 'counted' or 'credited' is what is meant by 'imputed', these passages, on their own, are conclusive:

> Abraham believed God, and it was *counted* to him *as righteousness*. Now to the one who works, his wages are not counted as a gift but as his due. And to the one who does not work but believes in him who justifies the ungodly, his faith is *counted as righteousness*, just as David also speaks of the blessing of the one to whom God *counts righteousness* apart from works... [God's] purpose was to make [Abraham] the father of all who believe without being circumcised, so that *righteousness* would be *counted* to them as well... His faith was *counted* to him *as righteousness* (Rom. 4:3-6,11,22).

> Abraham believed God, and it was *counted* to him *as righteousness* (Jas. 2:23).

As for Christ's part in this, we have Paul's words to the believers at Corinth. In his first letter he told them the amazing truth that Christ himself (Christ himself, please note, not 'merely' his work) is – has been made – their righteousness though their union with him:

You are in Christ Jesus, who became to us... righteousness... (1 Cor. 1:30).[1]

In his second letter, the apostle took this further, explaining that this was accomplished by God in a glorious exchange[2] between Christ and his elect:

For our sake he [that is, God the Father] made him [that is, Christ] to be sin who knew no sin, so that in him we might become the righteousness of God (2 Cor. 5:21).

Centuries before, in the days of the old covenant, Jeremiah had prophesied it:

Behold, the days are coming, declares the LORD, when I will raise up for David a righteous branch, and he shall reign as king and deal wisely, and shall execute justice and righteousness in the land. In his days Judah will be saved, and Israel will dwell securely. And this is the name by which he will be called: 'The Lord is our righteousness' (Jer. 23:5-6; see also Jer. 33:15-16).

As Paul experienced and testified of himself, his desire was:

...that I may gain Christ and be found in him, not having a righteousness of my own that comes from the law, but that which comes through faith in Christ, the righteousness from God that depends on faith (Phil. 3:8-9).

Very well. We have 'imputed righteousness', and this righteousness – *which is Christ himself* – is imputed at the point of faith to the believer in Christ, as a consequence of his union with the Redeemer. This is the justification by faith that Paul preached:

By [Christ] everyone who believes is justified from everything from which you could not be justified by the law of Moses (Acts 13:39).

But what, specifically, is this 'righteousness' which is imputed to the believing sinner? I am convinced that it is

---

[1] Once again we see that 'Christ is all' (Col. 3:11).
[2] See my 'The Glorious Exchange'.

Christ's life-long obedience under the law of God, the law given to Israel on Sinai through Moses. This is imputed to the sinner the moment he trusts Christ and is thus united to him.

I admit at once that there is no text which states as much. If this is a clinching argument, then, of course, end of story! But is it the clinching argument? If it is, then we will have problems with, say, justification by faith alone, since there is no text which states that doctrine.[3] Despite this lack of a single text, I still believe both. Both, to my mind, are revealed plainly in Scripture, even though no single text categorically states either.

Let me tackle an objection. What I have just said does *not* mean that I am starting with my theology or a Confession and coming to a conclusion; nor am I arguing that a theological system trumps the text of Scripture. Too often, I readily admit, these things happen.[4] But this is not what I am doing. No![5] Rather, I am claiming that Scripture itself, *taken as a whole*, inevitably leads to one conclusion on both topics; namely, that though they lack a single textual statement, both are scriptural.

If I may be permitted to make an objection of my own to the objector: it seems to me that some approach imputed righteousness rather as Little Jack Horner got stuck into his pie; they like to pull out a few plums from Scripture, and thus announce their doctrine. The right thing to do, however, is to devour the whole pie, down to the last crumb of the crust. I mean, of course, that to get a real grasp of the

---

[3] I can understand why Martin Luther felt the need to insert 'alone' in his German translation of Rom. 3:28, but he did it without the warrant of the Greek text.

[4] See my 'The Law and the Confessions'; 'A Must-See Debate'; 'No Confession? Nothing to Debate!'; 'Misleading, Sad, Revealing: "Relevant Today" by Jeremy Brooks'; 'Has it Really Come to This? Comments on a Banner Article: Part 1'; 'A Must-Listen Podcast'.

[5] To avoid this accusation, I have deliberately not given scores and scores of excellent extracts from Reformed authors.

righteousness which is imputed to the believer, we need to look at the big picture of Scripture, including the old covenant, and not confine ourselves to isolated passages, let alone texts, of the New Testament. I know I take a risk in saying this. I fully accept that it is 'to the law and to the testimony' (Isa. 8:20). And Acts 17:11 is still paramount. But this is the point! In both cases, it is the scrutiny of the entire Scripture, not isolated texts, that is commended as essential. 'What does the Scripture say?' (Rom. 4:3: Gal. 4:30). And when Christ spoke of searching the Scriptures (John 5:39), I am sure he did not intend us to grasp at verses, and miss the big picture.

Having said that, let me immediately add that my concern in writing on these matters is not confined to the text of Scripture. Please hear me out! I have a pastoral concern. Just as with justification by faith alone, so with the imputed righteousness of Christ: both carry huge consequences. The fact is, in each case I am concerned with the text of Scripture *and* the souls of men and women. Just as when the 'alone' is left out of 'justification by faith alone' the door is left ajar for, say, baptismal regeneration, so, without the imputed righteousness of Christ in the sense of his life-long obedience under the law, believers are bereft of massive scriptural comfort and assurance. What I am trying to say is that I am not engaging in an arid debate along the lines of cramming angels on pinheads. Rather, I am thinking of real people who have real needs, both in life and death, and trying to help them to come to a right understanding of Scripture.

To deny the imputation of Christ's life-long obedience under the law to the believer, and reducing justification to pardon, leaves us with what I can only describe as a one-legged gospel: the believer is washed from his sin, yes, but he is not clothed with righteousness. Righteousness! That's the word! So important is the concept, I must say a little more about it.

I start with a negative. Righteousness is not mere pardon; it is far more than that. Of the countless scriptural examples

Introduction

to make the point, consider the book of Proverbs. On my count, 'righteous' or 'righteousness' appears in seventy-five verses, and when words (and their derivatives) such as 'uprightness', 'integrity', 'godliness', and so on, are taken into account, the list grows rapidly. And the picture we are given of righteousness is always one of positive, practical living, not mere pardon. What is more, take some verses from just two consecutive chapters in the book of Proverbs – Proverbs 13:9,21,22,25; 14:9,11,19,32,34. These verses speak of a contrast, a clear – even stark – contrast between the righteous and the wicked (or their equivalents). The contrast is not between the righteous and the unpardoned, but between the righteous and the ungodly, the wicked, the sinful. Nothing could be clearer: righteousness is far more than pardon. And that comes from just two chapters in the book! On my reckoning, this contrast between the righteous and the wicked appears in over fifty verses throughout Proverbs. And if all the equivalents for 'righteous' and 'wicked' are taken into account, that number rises, I might almost say, exponentially.[6]

My point is that by saying that justification is pardon – by claiming that the righteousness imputed to the believer is mere pardon – we end up with a deformed, inadequate gospel. A believer, being justified, is pardoned, yes, but he is also positively righteous. David spoke of a man's sins being both pardoned and covered (Ps. 32:1; Rom. 4:7). 'Covered' is not a tautology, a mere repeat of 'pardon'. The Bible has a good deal to say on the subject of covering in this respect (see Job 29:14; Ps. 132:9; Isa. 11:5; 59:17; 61:10; 64:6; Zech. 3:4; Rev. 3:4; 19:8). The Greek in Romans 4:7 is *epikaluptō*, literally 'upon or over to hide, to veil', 'to cover over so as not to come to view'. See 1 Peter 2:6, where *epikalumma* is a cloak. Hence 'the wedding garment' (Matt. 22:11-14). I contend that the covering in question for the

---

[6] While 'pardon' and 'forgiveness' (and equivalents) are massive biblical concepts, the words themselves are not frequent in Scripture.

13

believer is nothing less than the robe of Christ's righteousness.

John Gill spoke of those:

> ...whom God justifies by imputing the righteousness of his Son to them, he removes their iniquities from them... such whom he clothes with the robe of righteousness, and garments of salvation (Isa. 61:10), 'their sins are covered' from the eye of divine justice, and shall never be seen [any] more, or be brought against them to their condemnation, and therefore [they] must be happy persons.

Again, to deny the imputation of Christ's life-long obedience under the law to the believer, leaves God's demand in the old covenant – 'Do this and live' (Lev. 18:5; Neh. 9:29; Ezek. 18:9; 20:11,13,21; Luke 10:26-28; Rom. 10:5; Gal. 3:12) – hanging in the air, unfulfilled. And this contradicts Matthew 5:17-18. Christ left nothing undone. He fully met God's just demands, keeping his commands to the jot and tittle. He came specifically to do his Father's will. His Father's law was in his heart (Ps. 40:7-8; Heb. 10:7,9). As he explained to the woman at the well, throughout his lifetime the Lord Jesus never forgot that he was about his Father's work and accomplishing it (John 4:34; see also John 5:30; 12:27; 17:4; 19:28). As he said: 'The Son of Man came not to be served but to serve, and to give his life as a ransom for many' (Mark 10:45). Yes, the culmination of his obedience was, without doubt, his *tetelestai* on the cross: 'It is finished' or 'It is accomplished' (John 19:30). But what was finished or accomplished? Not just his work on the cross!

I am convinced that the full glory of free justification lies in the fact that the life-long obedience of the Redeemer under the law is imputed to the believer. For this means that the believer, being united to Christ, has fully met all God's demands in his Saviour, and is therefore totally free of accusation, let alone condemnation (Rom. 8:1-4,33-34). He is fully pardoned and accounted perfectly righteousness in God's sight: 'Christ loved the church and gave himself up for her, that he might sanctify her, having cleansed her by the washing of water with the word, so that he might present the church to himself in splendour, without spot or wrinkle or any such thing, that she might be holy and without blemish' (Eph. 5:25-27). 'You, who once were alienated and hostile in mind, doing evil deeds, he has now reconciled in his body of flesh by his death, in order to present you holy and blameless and above reproach before him' (Col. 1:21-22; see also Rom. 7:4).[7] Yes, the believer is washed in Christ's blood and therefore pardoned (Heb. 9:14; 1 John 1:9), but he is also clothed in splendour, he is 'redeemed and purified' (Tit. 2:14; Heb. 1:3). In short, in Christ the saints are God's holy people (1 Pet. 2:9). In Christ they have completely satisfied the terms God laid out for Israel at Sinai:

> If you will indeed obey my voice and keep my covenant, you shall be my treasured possession among all peoples, for all the earth is mine; and you shall be to me a kingdom of priests and a holy nation (Ex. 19:5-6).

Without the imputed righteousness of Christ – his life-long obedience under the law – none of this would have been possible.

Indeed, it is only by stressing that the entire work of Christ in his life and death is the righteousness imputed to the believer, that Christ is given his full glory:

> Christ Jesus... though he was in the form of God, did not count equality with God a thing to be grasped, but emptied himself, by taking the form of a servant, being born in the likeness of men. And being found in human form, he humbled himself by becoming obedient to the point of death, even death on a cross. Therefore God has highly exalted him and bestowed on him the name that is above every name, so that at the name of Jesus every knee should bow, in heaven and on earth and under the earth, and every tongue confess that Jesus Christ is Lord, to the glory of God the Father (Phil. 2:3-11).

And so on...

---

[7] See my *Four*.

But I must not forget that this is supposed to be only the Introduction! So I will call a halt, and leave you to get on with the book.

Just a final caution, however: I began this Introduction by speaking of warmth, warmth in discussion since not all believers agree on this topic. It is gratifying when that warmth comes from hearts full of love, and not hot heads. After all, if we cannot in love discuss, of all subjects, the imputation of the work of Christ to the believer as the believer's righteousness, what hope is there for us?

Into the Lions' Den: Christ's Active Obedience Re-Visited

Definitions

Justification by faith is a legal or forensic term. The sinner who trusts Christ is justified; that is, God pardons the guilt of the sinner who trusts Christ, and imputes righteousness to him, constituting him perfect in his sight.

Christ's obedience is both *active* and *passive*.[1] Christ's *active* obedience is his entire life of obedience to his Father's will, including the Mosaic law, from his incarnation to his burial; his *passive* obedience is his suffering and death on the cross under the curse of the law.

To *impute* means to lay to the account of, to credit to. In justification, therefore, righteousness is laid to the account of, credited to, the sinner who believes.[2]

Righteousness in this context means perfection, uprightness.

And *justifying righteousness*, *Christ's righteousness*, is... Ah! That's what this article is about.

Introduction

When talking about justification, the phrase, 'Christ's righteousness', or its equivalent, appears repeatedly in countless books, hymns, sermons, Confessions of Faith, *etc.*,

---

[1] But, as I will explain, I do not like the terms. Nor do I agree with dividing Christ's obedience into distinct parts.

[2] There are, in fact, three imputations. *First*, Adam's guilt is imputed to all men (Ps. 51:5; Rom. 5:12,18-19; Eph. 2:1-3). *Secondly*, the sin of the elect is imputed to Christ (Isa. 53:4-6; Rom. 8:3-4; 2 Cor. 5:21; Gal. 3:13). *Thirdly*, Christ's righteousness is imputed to the elect (Rom. 3:21-26; 5:18-19; 2 Cor. 5:21; Phil. 3:9).

yet, remarkably, 'the righteousness of Christ', as a phrase, never once appears in Scripture. As may be imagined, many have held strong opinions about this expression, what it means, and whether or not it is right to use it. Needless to say, nobody – among those I am talking about – questions the sinlessness of Christ; *that* is not the point at issue. Rather, what is this 'righteousness', 'the righteousness of Christ', that God accounts to the sinner when he believes?

Here we come face to face with the much-debated topic of Christ's so-called active and passive obedience. In the matter of justification, I take 'the righteousness of Christ' to encompass both. In this article I briefly say why.

But before I do let me make it clear that, as I have noted, I do not like the terms 'active obedience' and 'passive obedience' when applied to the person and work of Christ. For a start, I do not approve of the notion of dividing the obedience of Christ; it is all one. Not only that. Christ was *active* on the cross, in his death. He could categorically state: 'I lay down my life that I may take it up again. No one takes it from me, but I lay it down of my own accord. I have authority to lay it down, and I have authority to take it up again. This charge I have received from my Father' (John 10:17-18). 'I lay down my life'! This is active! Again, as Christ asked Peter when he was being arrested, and Peter wanted to intervene by force: 'Shall I not drink the cup that the Father has given me?' (John 18:11). And his very dying was a voluntary act: 'Jesus, calling out with a loud voice, said: "Father, into your hands I commit my spirit!" And having said this he breathed his last' (Luke 23:46). Consequently, I would like to abandon this distinction between the 'active' and 'passive' obedience of Christ. 'Obedience', by definition, must an act of the will, a determined submission. Therefore, the notion that Jesus was active until the cross, and then passive, is utterly false. We know that right from the start Christ came to fulfil the law (Matt. 5:17).

Nevertheless, since the terms 'active' and 'passive' are used so frequently when talking about Christ's obedience, I am forced to fall in with the practice.

This question of whether or not Christ's active obedience is imputed to the sinner at the point of faith is, to say the least, contentious. Some say it is; others say it is not. And some have their say with vehemence. Good men are divided over it, strongly divided; indeed, I have friends on each side of the debate. Wisdom might dictate, therefore, that I should keep quiet, offend neither, and so preserve my good name with both. But I think it would be wrong of me not to set out a brief statement of my position. Even so, I know this article will disappoint (no worse than that, I hope!) some of my friends. Of course, I'm not foolish enough to think it is going to cut the Gordian knot. Yet it might help others think through the issue for themselves. Indeed, it might help me. For, if I am mistaken, I need to be shown it; constructive criticism of what I write could set me on the right path. I welcome such, therefore. I am not writing, as it were, with the inflated idea that I will bring all conversation on the subject to a close. Rather, I want to stimulate it.

Many things are not at issue, but what is at issue is this: What precisely is justification? What righteousness, precisely, is imputed to the believer for justification?

Before I start, a few negatives. Because of the sensitivity of this subject, I will quote no man's writing in support of what I say.[3] There is plenty to draw on, I assure you, but I refrain. I admit that too many base their case for including the active obedience of Christ in justification (as many other doctrines for that matter) on Confessions and the statements of good men. Parroting *Sola Scriptura* is all very well, but too often the reality is more akin to *Mainly* or *Primarily Confessional*. I will stick to Scripture.

Again, I do not take the position I do, in order to lend support to the advocates of covenant theology. But neither

---

[3] I do quote Martin Luther – but not to establish my thesis.

am I going to reject something which covenant theologians teach just because they do teach it. The fact is, whatever may be alleged, I do not take my stance because I am a covenant theologian, or because I am influenced by covenant theology, or because the vestiges of my long-held covenant theology colour my thinking here. Covenant theology has nothing to do with it, as far as I am concerned. In particular, I do not hold to the so-called covenant of works.[4] I am a new-covenant theologian. Even so, I do not approach the question because of my system; indeed, new-covenant theology is not a system such as, say, covenant theology. I have no system in mind other than to let Scripture speak.[5]

A common accusation laid against people like me is that we have a theory, and are hunting (in vain) for a text for it. I admit the obvious: there is no plain or explicit text for the inclusion of the active obedience of Christ in justification. Obvious? Of course! If there had been a plain text, there would be no debate. But if an explicit text is absolutely essential in forming doctrine, how will we establish – by an explicit text – that justification is by faith *alone*? Is there such a text? Again, is there an explicit text to prove that Christ, in his sufferings, earned the gift of faith for the elect?[6] What about the trinity, the pastor (if you hold to such an office), the canon of Scripture, the inclusion of the Song of Solomon in that canon, the cessation of the gifts, Jesus' establishment of Sunday as the Lord's day (if you think he did and think it is)? Can we be given a plain text for such? By the way, do not assume my opinion on any of these topics. I simply ask.

Justification is more than pardon

It seems to me that those who advocate passive obedience (and reject Christ's active obedience) in this matter of

---

[4] See my 'The Covenant That Never Was'.
[5] I acknowledge that I too have my presuppositions. We all do. But I *try* to argue my case from Scripture, not my theology.
[6] This is vital in the debate over Amyraldianism. See my *Amyraut*.

justification think that pardon, 'a clean slate', is the equivalent of justification. This is far too weak, and is, to speak frankly, unscriptural. The justified man is positively righteous in God's sight – not merely neutral, innocent, without guilt. He *is* pardoned, of course, but he is also perfect in God's sight – positively perfect, that is. I am deliberately using the tautology to make the point. It is not (merely) that his sins are forgiven: he is constituted righteous before God. Let me quote some relevant passages to make myself clear:

> As by the one man's disobedience the many were made sinners, so by the one man's obedience the many will be made righteous (Rom. 5:19).

Here we have it: by Christ's obedience, the believer is made or constituted 'righteous'. This is far more than being pardoned. Just as those in Adam are made more than merely 'sinful', so those in Christ are made more than merely 'un-sinful'.[7]

Again:

> In Christ God was reconciling the world to himself, not counting their trespasses against them... For our sake he made him to be sin who knew no sin, so that in him we might become the righteousness of God (2 Cor. 5:19-21).

Here we have it: in Christ believers are pardoned – God 'not counting their trespasses against them' – *and* fully righteous – they have become 'the righteousness of God' in Christ.

Again:

---

[7] It is commonly said that justification is 'just as if I had never sinned'. Not so! It is just as if I had always fully obeyed God in his law, and pleased him absolutely! And it is more that 'just as if'. In Christ, I *am* completely free of condemnation, having been made, constituted, perfectly righteous – as righteous and pleasing to God as Christ himself. It is not (as it is often said to be) that God (merely) declares me to be righteous. In Christ, he makes me righteous, he constitutes me a righteous man. See my *Four*.

21

We have been sanctified through the offering of the body of Jesus Christ once for all... For by a single offering he has perfected for all time those who are being sanctified (Heb. 10:10,14).[8]

Here we have it: by Christ's one offering,[9] the believer is made or constituted 'permanently perfect'. This is far more than being pardoned.

In the passage where he deals most extensively with the subject of justification (Rom. 1:16-17; 3:21– 5:21), the apostle is clear that righteousness is imputed to the believer; he is not merely pardoned. And that righteousness is called 'the righteousness of God' (Rom. 3:22), it being intimately connected with the person and work of Christ, and received through faith:

I am not ashamed of the gospel, for it is the power of God for salvation to everyone who believes, to the Jew first and also to the Greek. For in it the righteousness of God is revealed from faith for faith (Rom. 1:16-17).

---

[8] This 'perfection' speaks of the believer's positional sanctification and the 'sanctification' speaks of his progressive sanctification. The complication arises because of the translators and their use of 'sanctification'. The believer, as he trusts in Christ is counted 'perfect', fully righteous, in God's sight. Sanctification is both positional and progressive. By 'progressive sanctification', I mean the believer's imperfect (in this life) outworking of the perfect positional-sanctification he has in Christ by virtue of his union with Christ at his conversion. The sinner, on coming to faith, is united to Christ, and is justified and positionally sanctified. Thus, in God's sight, in Christ he is accounted or made righteous, free of sin and condemnation, and perfectly separated unto God. See, for instance, 1 Cor. 1:2,30; 6:11; Eph. 5:25-27; Heb. 10:10-18; 13:12. In his Christian life, he has to work out his perfection in Christ, and he will be moved to do so by the Spirit under the direction of Scripture; this is his progressive sanctification or holiness of life. But this, alas, is imperfect. The believer will only be absolutely sanctified in the eternal state. See my *Fivefold*.

[9] This, I grant, seems to clinch the case for the passive-obedience-only school. But if it were that simple, there would be no debate. Read on.

The righteousness of God has been manifested apart from the law... the righteousness of God through faith in Jesus Christ for all who believe... to show his righteousness at the present time, so that he might be just and the justifier of the one who has faith in Jesus (Rom. 3:21-22,26).

To the one who does not work but believes in him who justifies the ungodly, his faith is counted as righteousness (Rom. 4:5).

For if, because of one man's trespass, death reigned through that one man, much more will those who receive the abundance of grace and the free gift of righteousness reign in life through the one man Jesus Christ... As by the one man's disobedience the many were made sinners, so by the one man's obedience the many will be made righteous (Rom. 5:17,19).

And it is not only in Romans 1:16-17; 3:21 – 5:21 that we meet with such statements:

Gentiles who did not pursue righteousness have attained it, that is, a righteousness that is by faith (Rom. 9:30).

Christ is the end of the law for righteousness to everyone who believes (Rom. 10:4).

Christ Jesus, who became to us wisdom from God, righteousness and sanctification and redemption (1 Cor. 1:30).

We know that a person is not justified by works of the law but through faith in Jesus Christ, so we also have believed in Christ Jesus, in order to be justified by faith in Christ and not by works of the law, because by works of the law no one will be justified... For through the law I died to the law, so that I might live to God. I have been crucified with Christ. It is no longer I who live, but Christ who lives in me. And the life I now live in the flesh I live by faith in the Son of God, who loved me and gave himself for me. I do not nullify the grace of God, for if righteousness were through the law, then Christ died for no purpose (Gal. 2:16-21).

That I may gain Christ and be found in him, not having a righteousness of my own that comes from the law, but that

which comes through faith in Christ, the righteousness from
God that depends on faith (Phil. 3:8-9).

Although none of these passages use the phrase, 'the
righteousness of Christ', nevertheless that is precisely what
they are referring to – the righteousness which is imputed to
the sinner at the point of faith, the righteousness *of* God, a
righteousness *from* God, this righteousness being intimately
connected with Christ; in short, 'the righteousness of Christ'.
Now this righteousness cannot possibly be Christ's intrinsic
righteousness.[10] If it is, why did Christ have to become a

---

[10] Take 'the righteousness of God' in Rom. 1:16-17. On this,
Luther movingly commented: 'I had been captivated with a
remarkable ardour for understanding Paul in the epistle to the
Romans. But up until then it was... but a single saying... "In it the
righteousness of God is revealed" – that stood in my way. For I
hated that word "righteousness of God", which... I had been taught
to understand... the formal... justice... by which God is righteous
and punishes sinners and the unrighteous. Though I lived as a
monk without reproach, I felt I was a sinner before God with a
most disturbed conscience. I could not believe that he was placated
by my satisfaction. I did not love – indeed, I hated – the righteous
God who punishes sinners. Secretly, if not blasphemously,
certainly murmuring greatly, I was angry with God. Yet I clung to
the dear Paul and had a great yearning to know what he meant.
Finally, by the mercy of God, as I meditated day and night, I paid
attention to the context of the words: "In it the righteousness of
God is revealed, as it is written: 'He who through faith is righteous
shall live'". Then I began to understand that the righteousness of
God is that by which the righteous [man] lives by a gift of God,
namely by faith. This, then, is the meaning: the righteousness of
God is revealed by the gospel, *viz.*... the... righteousness with which
the merciful God justifies us by faith, as it is written: "The
righteous one lives by faith". Here I felt that I was altogether born
again and had entered paradise itself through open gates. There a
totally [different] face of all Scripture showed itself to me. And
whereas before "the righteousness of God" had filled me with hate,
now it became to me inexpressibly sweet in greater love. This
passage of Paul became to me a gateway to heaven' (see: 'Preface
to Latin Writings [1545]' in *Luther's Works* 34:336-37; WAusg
54.185-86).

man, live under the law and die on the cross? Then again, in his justification, the believing sinner is not so joined to Christ that he is 'Godified' or 'deified'; being a 'partaker of the divine nature' (see 2 Pet. 1:4) does not mean that![11] Nevertheless, he is constituted righteous. Whatever else can this righteousness, the righteousness of Christ, be, therefore, but Christ's complete mediatorial obedience to his Father's will, including the law of Moses, culminating in his sacrifice on the cross, all of which was vindicated by his resurrection?

Christ, himself, is the believer's righteousness

I have already quoted the apostolic assertion: 'Christ Jesus... became to us... righteousness' (1 Cor. 1:30). In his prophecy, Jeremiah, the prophet who more than any predicted the glory of the new covenant (Jer. 31:31-34; Heb. 8:6-13), made it clear that, in the new covenant, Christ himself would be the believer's righteousness:

> 'Behold, the days are coming', declares the Lord, 'when I will raise up for David a righteous Branch, and he shall reign as king and deal wisely, and shall execute justice and righteousness in the land. In his days Judah will be saved, and Israel will dwell securely. And this is the name by which he will be called: "The Lord is our righteousness"' (Jer. 23:5-6).

He repeated the point:

> 'Behold, the days are coming', declares the Lord, 'when I will fulfil the promise I made to the house of Israel and the house of Judah. In those days and at that time I will cause a righteous Branch to spring up for David, and he shall execute justice and righteousness in the land. In those days Judah will be saved, and Jerusalem will dwell securely. And this is the name by which it will be called: "The Lord is our righteousness"' (Jer. 33:14-16).

Christ *himself* is the believer's righteousness (Jer. 23:6; 33:16; 1 Cor. 1:30; 2 Pet. 1:1); that is, Christ and all his

---

[11] See also Heb. 3:14; 6:4.

work, his whole obedience, constitute the believer's righteousness. So much so, to crown it all, Christ himself is the new covenant (Isa. 42:6; 49:8).[12] Christ's obedience, Christ himself, throughout his life from his birth to his resurrection, culminating in his death, established this righteousness for his elect, which becomes theirs as they come to faith.

Take Philippians 3:8-11. Paul, speaking passionately of 'the righteousness which is from God by faith', explained his meaning: 'Righteousness... which is through faith in Christ, the righteousness which is from God by faith; that I may know him [Christ]'. That I may know *him*! That's it! This 'righteousness' that Paul needed and found could be summed up in a person: Christ! Christ himself!

And the same goes for every believer: Christ *himself* is the believer's righteousness. The believer is constituted righteous because he is united to Christ, because he is in Christ and Christ is in him. As a believer, Christ is formed in him, lives in him by the Spirit (John 14:23; 15:1-11; 17:23; Rom. 8:9-11; Gal. 2:20; 4:19; Eph. 3:17; Col. 1:27). The true believer must live as Jesus lived (see 1 John 2:6, NIV), and, by the Spirit, he is empowered to grow in Christ-likeness. 'As the living Father sent me, and I live because of the Father, so whoever feeds on me, he also will live because of me' (John 6:57). In how many ways Scripture highlights union with Christ! It is such an important concept. No wonder, then, that the phrase 'in Christ' appears so often in the sacred pages.

In short, the believer is righteous, righteous because he is in Christ and Christ is in him. Union with Christ, the believer's union with Christ in his life, death and resurrection, is the key (Rom. 6:1-14; Eph. 2:6).

We know that Christ came into the world expressly to do his Father's will (Heb. 10:5-10), and that included obedience to the will of God expressed in the Mosaic law. Christ, therefore, was born under the law (Gal. 4:4). As a

---

[12] For my view of this, see my *Believers*.

26

consequence, Christ, in his life, was fully obedient to the commands of the law, and, in his death, suffered its penalty, curse and condemnation. Throughout his life he was obedient to his Father, always pleasing him. As he himself said: 'I do nothing on my own authority, but speak just as the Father taught me... I always do the things that are pleasing to him' (John 8:28-29). Always! Not just in his dying on the cross! 'I lay down my life that I may take it up again. No one takes it from me, but I lay it down of my own accord. I have authority to lay it down, and I have authority to take it up again. This charge I have received from my Father' (John 10:17-18). 'I have not spoken on my own authority, but the Father who sent me has himself given me a commandment – what to say and what to speak... What I say, therefore, I say as the Father has told me' (John 12:49-50). 'I do as the Father has commanded me' (John 14:31). In this way, both actively and passively, Christ established that righteousness which would justify the elect. God the Father demonstrated his total satisfaction – pleasure – in, by and with this completed work of his Son, and his full acceptance of it, by raising him from the dead, receiving him back in exaltation into glory, crowned in triumph (Ps. 24:7-10; Isa. 52:13; 53:12; Phil. 2:9-11; 1 Tim. 3:16). And all this belongs to the believer because he is 'in Christ'.

Before I develop all this, let me say that there is no question but that the weight of Scripture comes down heavily on Christ's blood-sacrifice as God's justifying act (Rom. 3:24-26; 5:6,8-10; 6:1-10; 7:6; 8:3; 2 Cor. 5:18-21; Gal. 3:13; Heb. 9:12-15,28; 10:1-14; 13:12; 1 Pet. 3:18; and scores of others). As Paul told us, this is at the heart of the Lord's supper: 'For as often as you eat this bread and drink this cup, you proclaim the Lord's death till he comes' (1 Cor. 11:26). Above all, we have the cardinal text: 'As one trespass led to condemnation for all men, so one act of righteousness leads to justification and life for all men' (Rom. 5:18). That 'one act of righteousness' can only be Christ's sacrifice on the cross, the shedding of his blood. Scripture always lays massive emphasis on the death of

Christ, under the curse of the law, as the justifying righteousness which God accounts to the believer. And nothing I write here must, in the slightest way, be taken to indicate that I am in the least degree detracting from Christ's blood-sacrifice. *But this does not mean that Christ's life of obedience to the Father's will under the law of Moses had no place in establishing the believer's justifying righteousness.* Just as we must not detract from his blood-sacrifice, so must we not detract from his law-life of obedience. After all, as I have shown, justification is more than forgiveness, more than pardon; it is God accounting righteousness to the one to be justified. There is a negative aspect to all this: the removal of sin, its guilt, condemnation and power. But there is also a positive aspect: the reckoning of righteousness.

The Mosaic law's regulations fully typified this – the offering of a sacrificial victim. The shedding of its blood typified the removal of sin. The victim had to be without blemish (Ex. 12:5; 29:1; and scores more). Christ, fulfilling the law in every aspect, was without blemish (1 Pet. 1:19). His obedience under the law fitted him to be the perfect sacrifice (Heb. 5:9).[13]

Even so, there is more to Christ's life of obedience than to fit him to be the sacrifice. It did of course, but as he told John the Baptist when urging him to baptise him: 'Let it be so now, for thus it is fitting for us to fulfil all righteousness' (Matt. 3:15). In his baptism, Christ was identified with us. And this is part of his sanctifying of himself for us (John 17:18-19).

---

[13] And speaking of the sacrifices, in the first five chapters of Leviticus, we read of two types of offering under the old covenant: the sweet-savoured and the non-sweet. The latter typified the work of Christ in bearing both his people's guilt and God's wrath upon them for it; the former, his righteousness offered to justify them (Eph. 5:2). Thus, as in so many matters (sabbath, priesthood, sacrifice, temple, altar, feast, and so on), the old covenant was a shadow of the new.

And that was just the start of it. The Son of God became a man for the very purpose of living a life of obedience to the law, which obedience culminated in the offering of his body on the cross. And he underwent all this in order to establish the righteousness that would justify his people. True, the penalty of the law was death, but the way of righteousness under the law was: 'Do and live' (Lev. 18:5; Neh. 9:29; Ezek. 20:11,13,21; Rom. 10:5); as Moses declared to the Israelites: 'It will be righteousness for us, if we are careful to observe all these commandments before the LORD our God, as he has commanded us' (Deut. 6:25). '[God] will render to each one according to his works... It is not the hearers of the law who are righteous before God, but the doers of the law who will be justified' (Rom. 2:6,13). The law was 'the very commandment that promised life' (Rom. 7:10), 'the very commandment that was intended to bring life' (NIV), 'which was to result in life' (NASB). That is to say, if a man kept God's law perfectly, he would merit life – eternal life.[14] In other words, the law had two things to say with regard to sin and righteousness: it issued both precept and penalty. On the one hand, it demanded perfect obedience and promised reward for it, while, on the other hand, it warned and exacted the ultimate penalty for one transgression. Hence, instead of saying that God demanded 'active' and 'passive' obedience to the law, we could speak in terms of 'preceptive' and 'penal' obedience. Christ suffered the penalty of disobedience (though he himself never sinned) (Isa. 53:1-10; Gal. 3:13), and obtained the reward for perfect obedience (Isa. 53:10-12; John 13:31-32; 17:1).

It was for this very reason, as I have said, that Christ was born under the law (Gal. 4:4). This means far more than that he was a Jew. He was, of course, but he was born under the law in order to come under its jurisdiction, and obey it and suffer under it so that he might redeem his people (Gal. 4:5). And this he did perfectly, without sin (2 Cor. 5:21; Heb.

---

[14] Of course, because man is fallen in Adam, the law cannot justify; it is too weak for that (Rom. 8:3).

29

4:15; 7:26), thus earning salvation for his people – his entire obedience culminating in the offering of himself (or the Father's offering of his Son) as a perfect, spotless sacrifice on the cross. He became, therefore, the perfect Saviour for sinners for ever (Heb. 2:10,18; 5:9; 7:28). His entire existence as a man leading up to the cross is also a vital and integral part of this 'righteousness of Christ'. Hence:

> Mary... will bring forth a son, and you shall call his name Jesus, for he will save his people from their sins (Matt. 1:20-21). God was manifested in the flesh (1 Tim. 3:16). The Word became flesh and dwelt among us (John 1:14). Jesus Christ... was born of the seed of David according to the flesh (Rom. 1:3). You know the grace of our Lord Jesus Christ, that though he was rich, yet for your sakes he became poor, that you through his poverty might become rich (2 Cor. 8:9). When the fullness of the time had come, God sent forth his Son, born of a woman, born under the law, to redeem those who were under the law... (Gal. 4:4-5). Christ Jesus, who, being in the form of God, did not consider it robbery to be equal with God, but made himself of no reputation, taking the form of a bondservant, and coming in the likeness of men. And being found in appearance as a man, he humbled himself and became obedient to the point of death, even the death of the cross... (Phil. 2:5-8). Inasmuch then as the children have partaken of flesh and blood, he himself likewise shared in the same [their humanity – NIV], that through death he might destroy him who had the power of death, that is, the devil, and release those who through fear of death were all their lifetime subject to bondage (Heb. 2:14-15). When he came into the world, he said: '...A body you have prepared for me... "Behold, I have come... to do your will, O God"...'... By that will we have been sanctified through the offering of the body of Jesus Christ once for all (Heb. 10:5-10).

When he was twelve, Jesus told his parents that he must be 'about [his] Father's business' (Luke 2:49). And, as we have seen, when he came to John to be baptised, he spoke of fulfilling 'all righteousness' (Matt. 3:15). While we must avoid speculation, we may surely say that, right from his baptism, the Lord Jesus was on that path of public obedience which would lead him inexorably to the cross. And in the years following his baptism, right up to his crucifixion, how often he spoke of the will of his Father, of his doing that will, of his finishing the work his Father had given him to do (John 4:34; 5:30; 6:38; 9:4; 17:4), culminating in his triumphant cry on the cross: 'It is finished' (John 19:30). Truly, as a 'servant' (Isa. 42:1; 52:13; Matt. 20:28; Phil. 2:7), Christ always kept his vow to his Father (Ps. 40:6–8; Heb. 10:5-9). And God was pleased. So much so, in prophecy Christ could say:

> He brought me out into a broad place; he rescued me, because he delighted in me. The Lord dealt with me according to my righteousness; according to the cleanness of my hands he rewarded me. For I have kept the ways of the Lord, and have not wickedly departed from my God. For all his rules were before me, and his statutes I did not put away from me. I was blameless before him, and I kept myself from my guilt. So the Lord has rewarded me according to my righteousness, according to the cleanness of my hands in his sight (Ps. 18:19-24).

Consequently, although Scripture lays heavy stress on the death of Christ, the shedding of his blood in atoning sacrifice, as the justifying act, it also speaks of his obedience (Phil. 2:8; Heb. 5:8-9; 10:5-14,19-20). 'By one man's obedience many will be made [constituted] righteous' (Rom. 5:19). Without question, this obedience, as I said, culminated in his death (Matt. 26:39; John 10:18; Rom. 5:18-19; Phil. 2:8; Heb. 5:8; 10:10), for 'Christ... offered himself without spot' – 'without blemish' (NASB); 'unblemished' (NIV) – 'to God' (Heb. 9:14). Nevertheless, his life-obedience was essential to that work. When we are told that God sent 'his own Son in the likeness of sinful flesh and for sin [and thus] he condemned sin in the flesh, in order that the righteous requirement of the law might be fulfilled in us' (Rom. 8:3-4), we must not restrict this to Christ's work on the cross, but include his entire life of obedience.

Furthermore, we know that Christ is 'the last Adam' (1 Cor. 15:45). The first Adam failed to obey God, and therefore died, bringing all men down with him by his one act of disobedience, his one sin, his one trespass (Rom. 5:16,18), resulting in a cataract of trespasses (Rom. 5:16), and the reign of death (Rom. 5:17). Christ, 'the last Adam', lived a life of perfect obedience to God his Father, and then offered that perfect life in his one and only sacrificial death to atone for the elect, thus uniting his active and passive obedience in order to present his people faultless before his Father, enabling them to reign in life (Rom. 5:17), even as kings (1 Pet. 2:4-10; Rev. 1:6; 5:10; 20:6).

Yes, the apostle does speak of Adam and Christ in terms of 'one act' – Adam's one act of disobedience and Christ's 'one act of righteousness' (Rom. 5:18). But there is a contrast which must not be missed. To ruin all and bring the threatened condemnation, one transgression was sufficient; to merit the promised reward, a lifetime of obedience was required. Just as: 'Whoever keeps the whole law but fails in one point has become accountable for all of it' (Jas. 2:10), so to obtain the reward, Christ never once sinned throughout his entire life. One transgression would have ruined all. Consequently, his entire life had to be one of complete obedience.

And then, to crown it all, Christ's entire obedience of life unto death was completely vindicated by his resurrection:

> Christ Jesus, who, being in the form of God, did not consider it robbery to be equal with God, but made himself of no reputation, taking the form of a bondservant, and coming in the likeness of men. And being found in appearance as a man, he humbled himself and became obedient to the point of death, even the death of the cross. Therefore God also has highly exalted him and given him the name which is above every name... (Phil. 2:5-9).

Now it is far too weak to say that Christ was raised from the dead simply to vindicate his work, or give proof of the justification he had accomplished on the cross, or to demonstrate that God was being fair to Christ in that since he had earned the pardon, so it was only right that he should be raised. The apostle used *dia*, 'for', 'on account of', in both parts of the following sentence. Christ was delivered *dia* our offences, and was raised *dia* our justification:

> Righteousness... shall be imputed to us who believe in him who raised up Jesus our Lord from the dead, who was delivered up because of [for] our offences, and was raised because of [for] our justification (Rom. 4:22-25; see also Rom. 8:33-34; 1 Cor. 15:17; 2 Cor. 5:15).

The apostle clearly attributes the same weight and power to the resurrection as he does to the death of Christ as far as justification goes. Christ died for our sins, on account of our sins, to deal with our sins, in order to deliver us from our offences, and likewise he was raised for our justification, on account of our justification, in order to justify us. This passage, on its own, drives a coach and horses through the passive-obedience-only view.[15]

I spoke of the resurrection, and the part it plays in justification. How frequently the early preachers included the resurrection! See Acts 2:24,31-33; 3:15,26; 4:2,10,33; 5:30-31; 10:40; 13:30,33-37; 17:3,18,31-32; 23:6; 24:15,21. In addition, I quote the following from my *Particular Redemption and The Free Offer*:

> Christ died *for* sinners and was raised again *for* those same sinners (Rom. 4:25 AV, NIV). *For* whom? Paul could tell believers: 'If Christ is not risen... you are still in your sins' (1 Cor. 15:17). 'But God, who is rich in mercy, because of his great love with which he loved us, even when we were dead in trespasses, made us alive together with Christ... and raised us up together, and made us sit together in the heavenly places in Christ Jesus' (Eph. 2:4-6). Christ died *for* – and was raised *for* – the elect, 'for us'. Not only so. The elect died *with* – and were raised *with* – Christ. This takes us to the vital doctrine of union and identification with Christ in his death *and* burial *and* resurrection *and* ascension. The elect died with Christ when he died, *and* were buried with him when he was buried, *and* were raised

---

[15] Union is the key, I remind you, and union with Christ involves union with him in his resurrection (Rom. 6:4-8).

with him when he was raised, *and* were taken into glory and seated with him (Rom. 6:2-11; 7:4-6; 2 Cor. 5:14-18; Gal. 2:19-20; Eph. 2:1,4-6; Col. 2:11-15,20; 3:1,3; 1 Pet. 2:24; see also John 14:19; Rom. 8:34; 1 Thess. 5:10; 1 Pet. 1:3). Christ 'was delivered up because of our offences, *and was raised for our justification*' (Rom. 4:25), the 'our' being, of course, the elect.[16]

Thus, Christ's *entire* work in his obedient life, culminating in his atoning sacrifice, leading to his vindication by the resurrection, all combined to weave that robe of righteousness which justifyingly clothes the believer in the sight of God (Isa. 61:10; Zech. 3:4). Moreover, as the apostle declared – and note the double 'much more' – 'much more then, having now been justified by his blood, we shall be saved from wrath through him. For if when we were enemies we were reconciled to God through the death of his Son, much more, having been reconciled, we shall be saved by his life' (Rom. 5:9-10); that is, in his resurrected life.[17]

Consider: 'Christ also has loved us and given himself for us, an offering and a sacrifice to God for a sweet-smelling aroma' (Eph. 5:2). Without doubt, the apostle is referring to the sacrificial death of Christ at Calvary. Now look at the context – both immediate and extended (Eph. 4:17 – 6:24). Once again, there is no question; the context is progressive sanctification. Let me quote the verse *in full*: 'And walk in love, as Christ also has loved us and given himself for us, an offering and a sacrifice to God for a sweet-smelling aroma'. 'Walk' is a word of progressive sanctification, practical godliness. The apostle is commanding believers to live a life of love, not only *because* Christ loved them and gave himself for them, but *as* – *even as, just as* – he loved them and gave himself for them. Believers must live as Christ

---

[16] My *Particular* pp28-29.

[17] Please note that I do not, as many, warp this to argue that this 'life' speaks of Christ's life before the cross, thereby forcing the text to support my thesis. Even so, it does show that Scripture can speak of Christ's work and life, other than on the cross, as contributing to our salvation.

lived before his death. In light of the point I am making, this tells me that Christ's obedience, while it was supremely his sacrificial *death*, also included his peerless *life*. In other words, 'the righteousness of Christ', which is accounted to the believer for justification, embraces Christ's entire obedience – both in life and death, both active and passive. Indeed, as I have observed, it is impossible to divide Christ's obedience in this way; it is all of a piece.[18]

Whatever the rights and wrongs of the note at the end of the previous paragraph, it is my conviction that Christ's lifetime obedience to his Father's will, including his obedience under the Mosaic law, culminating in his sacrificial death, all under the law, constitutes the justifying righteousness for believers – 'the righteousness of Christ'. And this is what is imputed to the believer.

Imputed righteousness

And when the sinner believes – trusts Christ – he receives this perfect righteousness of Christ. It is imputed to him. It is reckoned to him. It is credited to his account. He receives it at once. Upon his believing, he is absolutely justified. This righteousness, being Christ's perfect and unchangeable and unchanging righteousness, never wanes, never alters. It is fixed, absolute, complete, and knows no variation. The perfect righteousness of Christ clothes the believing sinner, and the believing sinner, therefore, is for ever, from the

---

[18] While I am, myself, firmly convinced that 'the faith *of* Christ' (Rom. 3:22,26; Gal. 2:16, twice; 3:22; Eph. 3:12; Phil. 3:9; all in the Greek) should be thought of as 'faith *in* Christ' (as NKJV, NIV, NASB – but see NASB margin in Rom. 3:26; Eph. 3:12), and not 'the faith *of* Christ' (AV – except Rom. 3:26), I realise that the point has been debated for centuries, and is still fervently contested today, not least in the debate over the New Perspective. If the 'of' is right – and, as I say, I am not persuaded it is; in fact, I am convinced that it is not – then perhaps 'the faith of Christ' could be thought of as 'the faithfulness of Christ'. As such, it would lend even more weight to the claim for justification by Christ's obedience in life, as well as his obedience in death.

instant he is justified, perfect beyond all condemnation in the sight of God. God sees no sin in him at all. I am not for a moment suggesting that the believer is sinless. I am not talking about progressive sanctification! No! I am concerned here with justification. I am not talking about the sinner's lifestyle, but his standing before God.[19] As the sinner believes, he is at once and for ever free of condemnation, whoever might accuse him, and whatever offence they might accuse him of (Rom. 8:1,33-34). *Christ* is his righteousness! Thus the gospel can truly be said to 'establish the law' (Rom. 3:31). All the law's commands were fully met by Christ. All the law's penalties were fully paid by Christ. All the Father's will was accomplished (John 19:30) by Christ who fulfilled the prophet's words: 'The LORD is well pleased for his righteousness' sake; he will exalt the law and make it honourable' (Isa. 42:21).

And this is what I understand by 'the righteousness of Christ', and the imputation of that righteousness to the sinner as he believes.

Finally, to make the point yet again

First:

> There is therefore now no condemnation for those who are in Christ Jesus. For the law of the Spirit of life has set you free in Christ Jesus from the law of sin and death. For God has done what the law, weakened by the flesh, could not do. By sending his own Son in the likeness of sinful flesh and for sin, he condemned sin in the flesh, *in order that the righteous requirement of the law might be fulfilled in us*, who walk not according to the flesh but according to the Spirit (Rom. 8:1-4).

---

[19] I am not saying, I hasten to add, that there is no connection between the two. Progressive sanctification is an inevitable consequence of justification. See Eph. 2:8-10, for example. See also Col. 1:22-23. No progressive sanctification? No justification! See Heb. 12:14; Jas. 2:14-26.

By Christ's work, 'the righteous requirement of the law' is 'fulfilled in us'; that is, in believers. 'Fulfilled', and 'fulfilled in us'! Clearly, this is something which God in Christ has done *for* and *in* believers, not something to be done *by* believers trying to keep the law. Paul here *describes* believers; he does not tell them to fulfil the law, spelling out their duty. God, by his Son, Christ Jesus, accomplished the fulfilment of the righteous requirement of the law, and it is this perfect obedience of Christ, his righteousness, which is imputed and imparted to believers. Thus Christ fulfilled the law, and believers have fulfilled it in him. Christ's work imputed to them by the Spirit accomplishes their justification. Christ's work being imparted to them by the Spirit accomplishes their progressive sanctification. And it is this sanctification which is the evidence and fruit of the fulfilment of the righteous requirement of the law in believers in and by Christ.

Note how Paul does not say the law is now 'obeyed' or 'kept' or 'done' by believers – the usual way of talking about keeping the law – but he says that what the law requires is now 'fulfilled' in believers. Note the passive. Note the word itself: 'fulfilled'! – a word of immense significance in New Testament terms. As we have seen, Christ set the tone right at the start: 'Do not think that I came to destroy the law or the prophets. I did not come to destroy but to fulfil. For assuredly, I say to you, till heaven and earth pass away, one jot or one tittle will by no means pass from the law till all is fulfilled' (Matt. 5:17-18). As Paul said in Galatians 5:13-18, the indwelling Spirit ensures the 'fulfilment' of the law, its goal, end or aim in the believer – which is, to bring about righteousness. The law, though holy, righteous and good (Rom. 7:12), being weak, could not bring about the righteousness that God required. It is the Spirit who has been given to believers in order to effect, to 'fulfil', the law in them, and so establish that righteousness which the law demanded but was unable to produce. The point is, 'the righteousness requirement' of the law demands positive obedience and not (mere) passive suffering. God 'passed over' the sins of Israel in the Passover, he did not visit them in wrath (Ex. 12:1-28). But the death of the sacrificial lamb did not make the Israelites positively righteous in God's sight. Christ our Passover has been sacrificed for us (1 Cor. 5:7), and so, while we have been redeemed by his precious blood (1 Pet. 1:19), our sins have been expiated, yet this still leaves the need for the imputation of positive righteousness. And we know what the law demanded; we have the scriptural mantra regarding the law: 'Do and live; fail to do and die':

> You shall follow my rules and keep my statutes and walk in them. I am the Lord your God. You shall therefore keep my statutes and my rules; if a person does them, he shall live by them: I am the Lord (Lev. 18:4-5).

> And behold, a lawyer stood up to put [Jesus] to the test, saying: 'Teacher, what shall I do to inherit eternal life?' He said to him: 'What is written in the law? How do you read it?' And he answered: 'You shall love the Lord your God with all your heart and with all your soul and with all your strength and with all your mind, and your neighbour as yourself'. And he said to him: 'You have answered correctly; do this, and you will live' (Luke 10:25-28).

> When [a man] has done what is just and right, and has been careful to observe all my statutes, he shall surely live. The soul who sins shall die... If a wicked person turns away from all his sins that he has committed and keeps all my statutes and does what is just and right, he shall surely live; he shall not die. None of the transgressions that he has committed shall be remembered against him; for the righteousness that he has done he shall live (Ezek. 18:19-22).

> [God] will render to each one according to his works: to those who by patience in well-doing seek for glory and honour and immortality, he will give eternal life; but for those who are self-seeking and do not obey the truth, but obey unrighteousness, there will be wrath and fury. There will be tribulation and distress for every human being who does evil, the Jew first and also the Greek, but glory and honour and peace for everyone who does good, the Jew first

and also the Greek. For God shows no partiality... It is not the hearers of the law who are righteous before God, but the doers of the law who will be justified (Rom. 2:6-11,13).

Moses writes about the righteousness that is based on the law, that the person who does the commandments shall live by them (Rom. 10:5).

All who rely on works of the law are under a curse; for it is written: 'Cursed be everyone who does not abide by all things written in the book of the law, and do them'. Now it is evident that no one is justified before God by the law, for: 'The righteous shall live by faith'. But the law is not of faith, rather: 'The one who does them shall live by them' (Gal. 3:10-12).

And then this:

Do not think that I have come to abolish the law or the prophets; I have not come to abolish them but to fulfil them. For truly, I say to you, until heaven and earth pass away, not an iota, not a dot, will pass from the law until all is accomplished. Therefore whoever relaxes one of the least of these commandments and teaches others to do the same will be called least in the kingdom of heaven, but whoever does them and teaches them will be called great in the kingdom of heaven. For I tell you, unless your righteousness exceeds that of the scribes and Pharisees, you will never enter the kingdom of heaven (Matt. 5:17-20).

And then:

Christ is the end of the law for righteousness to everyone who believes (Rom. 10:4).

Jesus was unique in that he is the only man that has ever lived in order to fulfil the will of God, and that will surely included the keeping and fulfilling of the law. Christ came into the world in order to fulfil it, as he said (Heb. 10:5-9), and he is the only man ever to come with that purpose, and to do it. Since we ourselves can never produce any better righteousness that that of the Pharisees, the only way that our righteousness can exceed theirs is if the righteousness of Jesus is imputed to us. Moreover, Matthew 5:17-20 speaks of far more than *suffering*, even unto *death*, under the law. Indeed, there is no suggestion whatsoever here of any connection between the Pharisees and death. It is all a question of *obedience* in *life*. Clearly, Christ was talking of positive obedience to the law.

In short, for justification the sinner has to have a righteousness which matched 'do and live', or else he would die. Christ did both the doing and the dying. It seems to me that the passive-obedience-only school captures the sense of the dying and the pardon, but the full biblical position is only reached if we include Christ's active obedience. We then get both the doing and the dying.

Conclusion

Whether, in this article, I have convinced anyone that we should think of both the active and passive obedience of Christ when speaking of justifying righteousness, such is my case. Nevertheless, as I have said, I am open to correction, and I welcome constructive criticism. I also respectfully ask those who still hold the passive-only-obedience position to face a few questions:

1. Is justification pardon or does it include positive righteousness?

2. If the answer to that question is the latter, then what, *precisely*, is this positive righteousness which is imputed to the believer?

3. Have you taken *full* account of both the *parallel* and the *contrast* involved in Paul's comparison of Adam and Christ?

4. Why, on your scheme, did Jesus have to become a Jew, to be made under the law?

5. Have you taken *full* account of Romans 4:25?

6. In light of that question, do you regard the life of Christ merely a preparation for the cross, and his resurrection

40

merely a vindication of the cross? Or does Christ's life and justification play a bigger role in the believer's justification than you allow?

Observations on a Colloquy

The colloquy in question is the In-Depth Studies Colloquy: 'Is the Cross Alone Sufficient for Salvation?', which was held on the 29th of April 2017 at the Gilbert Regional Library, Phoenix.1 Brian Arnold took the 'No' position and Geoff Volker took the 'Yes'.

The issue under debate was the old question of Christ's active/passive obedience. Is Christ's life of obedience under the law imputed to those who believe, so that the justified sinner is both cleansed from his sin in the blood of Christ (in simple terms, the passive obedience of Christ) and accounted righteous, made positively righteousness, having received the imputation of Christ's perfect obedience under the law (in simple terms, the active obedience of Christ)? Brian argued 'Yes'; Geoff argued 'No'.

I want to make a very brief response. And I mean brief. Having already written on this subject,[2] I will only touch on what I see as a few key points raised by the colloquy.

To avoid all misunderstanding, let me say at once that I wholeheartedly agree with both Brian and Geoff that this is an in-house debate between brothers. This is not a wrangle. I publish this article entirely in accord with this spirit.

Again, as the two men agreed, there are many issues here which are held in common. We all believe in imputation. We all believe that Christ lived a perfect life, fulfilling all righteousness under the law, and we believe that this perfection was absolutely necessary in order that he might be an unblemished sin-offering on the cross. We also agree that the terms 'active obedience' and 'passive obedience' are, in some ways, unhelpful, since Christ was active on the cross in his so-called passive obedience. Nevertheless, we are stuck with these terms, and so we have to get on with it. But, to contradict myself a little, since it is agreed that Christ was actively

---

[1] It may be found at the following link:
https://www.youtube.com/watch?v=j8B6rXRFBNA
[2] See my 'Into the Lions' Den: Christ's Active Obedience Re-Visited'.

43

obeying his Father on the cross, this, it seems to me, means that it is wrong to dismiss all talk of Christ's active obedience. So, these key points that I spoke about...

'Active obedience is a theological, not a biblical, construct'

I am, of course, quoting one of Geoff's arguments. Let me say at once that Geoff has put his finger on what I consider to be a major issue. In all sorts of areas, far too many believers read the Bible and interpret it in terms of a Confession or systematic theology. They wrest Scripture to fit their system. Let me give a couple of examples of the sort of thing I mean, issues that I have written about, and done so extensively:

1. Election, particular redemption and the free offer of the gospel.
2. The covenants, the law and the believer.

In both of these areas, far too many read the Bible to make it fit their system, rather than the other way about. The results of this tinkering with Scripture are disastrous. We must let God be true and (if necessary) every man and his Confession or system fall. Of course, nearly everybody will agree with the sentiment, but, as I say, in practice far too many work the other way round: Scripture is distorted to fit the system.

Is this the case with 'the active obedience of Christ'? If it is, if Scripture is distorted to make it fit a system, then the concept should be abandoned forthwith.

But there is a difference between 'biblical' and 'textual'. We all agree that there is no specific text which states that 'the active obedience of Christ, his perfect obedience to the law, is imputed to sinners when they believe'. No! But does this mean that we must, therefore, abandon the concept? Before we do, let us try the notion on one or two other topics.

Is there a specific text which states that the Godhead is One in Three persons? No!

Is there a specific text that states that the sinner is justified by faith alone? No!

Is there a specific text that states that believers are under the law of Christ? No![3]

Shall we, therefore, abandon the doctrine of the trinity, the doctrine of the justification of believers by faith alone, and the claim that believers are under the law of Christ? No! For all three are *biblical* doctrines even though they are not *textual* doctrines.

The question is of course: Is the imputation of Christ's active obedience a biblical doctrine? I assert that it is, but I will not argue the case here, having already done so in my aforementioned article.

'Justification is forgiveness'

This, it seems to me, is where Geoff ends up.

But is justification simply forgiveness? Or, as it came out in the colloquy, is the righteousness imputed to the believer defined as 'cleansing' or 'a clean slate'? Let me say immediately that by asking this question I intend no disparagement of forgiveness. How could I? It features so largely in the apostolic writings. But is the righteousness imputed to the believer limited to 'cleansing' or 'a clean slate'?

I think not. Notice Paul's direct comparison – better, contrast – of 'a righteousness... that comes from the law' with 'that which comes through faith in Christ, the righteousness from God that depends on faith' (Phil. 3:9); that is, through Christ. Does he mean '*a clean slate...* that comes from the law' with 'that which comes through faith in Christ, the *clean slate* from God that depends on faith'?

When Paul declares: 'For our sake [God] made him to be sin who knew no sin, so that in him we might become the righteousness of God' (2 Cor. 5:21), are we to limit this 'righteousness' to forgiveness? In other words: 'For our sake [God] made him to be sin who knew no sin, so that in him we might become [or have] *the clean slate* of God'?

---

[3] The original of 1 Cor. 9:21 does *not* state it! I agree with the translators, of course, who have translated it that way (see my *Believers*), but the point is, strictly speaking, it is not a textual phrase.

When Paul says that 'the righteousness of God has been manifested apart from the law... the righteousness of God through faith in Jesus Christ for all who believe... his righteousness... so that he might be just and the justifier of the one who has faith in Jesus' (Rom. 3:21-26), are we to understand this as forgiveness, the imputation of 'a clean slate' to the believer? That is: '*The clean slate* of God has been manifested apart from the law... *the clean slate* of God through faith in Jesus Christ for all who believe... his *clean slate*... so that he might be just and the justifier of the one who has faith in Jesus'?

When the apostle asserts that 'to the one who works, his wages are not counted as a gift but as his due. And to the one who does not work but believes in him who justifies the ungodly, his faith is counted as righteousness, just as David also speaks of the blessing of the one to whom God counts righteousness apart from works' (Rom. 4:4-6), was he referring merely to forgiveness, 'a clean slate'? That is: 'To the one who works, his wages are not counted as a gift but as his due. And to the one who does not work but believes in him who justifies the ungodly, his faith is counted as *a clean slate*, just as David also speaks of the blessing of the one to whom God counts *a clean slate* apart from works'?[4]

---

[4] While in Rom. 3:21 – 5:21 Paul does not define righteousness so as to include obedience to the law, but does speak of forgiveness (Rom. 4:7-8), this does not mean that righteousness is only forgiveness. After all, Paul has already said – and only just said – that 'it is not the hearers of the law who are righteous before God, but the doers of the law who will be justified' (Rom. 2:13). I am not saying that the believer is justified by his own obedience to the law, of course, but I am saying that the believer's righteousness does involve that perfect obedience to the law which was wrought for him by Christ. When we read 'righteousness' in Rom. 3 and beyond, therefore, this must be borne in mind. Consider: 'Gentiles who did not pursue righteousness have attained it, that is, a righteousness that is by faith; but that Israel who pursued *a law that would lead to righteousness* did not succeed in reaching that law. Why? Because they did not pursue it by faith, but as if it were based on works... Being ignorant of the righteousness of God, and seeking to establish their own, they did not submit to God's righteousness. For Christ is the end of the law for righteousness to everyone who believes. For Moses writes about *the righteousness that is based on the law*, that the person who does the commandments shall live by them. But the righteousness based on faith

And when Paul links 'obedience' (works) and 'righteousness' – as he does: 'For as by the one man's disobedience the many were made sinners, so by the one man's obedience the many will be made righteous' (Rom. 5:19) – surely he was thinking of more than forgiveness, 'a clean slate', was he not? Or are we to think in terms of this: 'For as by the one man's disobedience the many were made sinners, so by the one man's obedience the many will be given *a clean slate*'?

When Paul speaks of 'the weapons of righteousness for the right hand and for the left' (2 Cor. 6:7; see also Eph. 6:10-17; 1 Thess. 5:8) for the servants of God, is he referring to the weapons of *a clean slate*?[5]

And turning to the old covenant, the Mosaic law – the law under which Christ lived and died – surely the reward for law-keeping was more than forgiveness, 'a clean slate', was it not? Does this not play into: 'Christ is the end of the law for righteousness to everyone who believes' (Rom. 10:4)? 'Christ is the end of the law for *a clean slate* to everyone who believes'?

Let us apply the suggestion to Romans 4, Abraham and the believer. Are we to read Scripture like this:

---

says...' (Rom. 9:30 – 10:6). It is the same point. Righteousness under the law and under the gospel both involve obedience to the law. The law promised life (Rom. 7:10) for perfect obedience. As Christ said: 'Do this [the law], and you will live' (Luke 10:28). Israel could say: 'It will be righteousness for us, if we are careful to do all this commandment before the Lord our God, as he has commanded us' (Deut. 6:25). In the old covenant, the righteousness had to be the sinner's own obedience – impossible. In the new covenant, the sinner's righteousness is Christ's obedience on his behalf. See below for Rom. 8 and Rom. 10.

[5] John Calvin: 'By "righteousness" you must understand rectitude of conscience, and holiness of life'. John Gill: 'By the armour of righteousness, on the right hand, and on the left: meaning, either the whole armour of God, with which a Christian is all over clothed from head to foot, and in the strength of Christ may engage any adversary without fear; or else particularly the sword of the Spirit in the right hand, and the shield of faith in the left, whereby both the offensive and defensive part may be acted; or, as others think, uprightness of conscience, and holiness of life and conversation'.

If Abraham was justified by works, he has something to boast about, but not before God. For what does the Scripture say? 'Abraham believed God, and it was counted to him as *a clean slate*'. Now to the one who works, his wages are not counted as a gift but as his due. And to the one who does not work but believes in him who justifies the ungodly, his faith is counted as *a clean slate*... He received the sign of circumcision as a seal of *the clean slate* that he had by faith while he was still uncircumcised. The purpose was to make him the father of all who believe without being circumcised, so that *a clean slate* would be counted to them as well... the promise to Abraham and his offspring that he would be heir of the world did not come through the law but through *the clean slate* of faith... his faith was 'counted to him as *a clean slate*'. But the words 'it was counted to him' were not written for his sake alone, but for ours also. It will be counted to us who believe in him who raised from the dead Jesus our Lord, who was delivered up for our trespasses and raised for our *clean slate* (Rom. 4)?

Really?

And how about Romans 8:1-4? Is this what Paul meant us to understand:

There is therefore now no condemnation for those who are in Christ Jesus. For the law of the Spirit of life has set you free in Christ Jesus from the law of sin and death. For God has done what the law, weakened by the flesh, could not do. By sending his own Son in the likeness of sinful flesh and for sin, he condemned sin in the flesh, in order that the righteous requirement of the law – namely, *a clean slate* – might be fulfilled in us, who walk not according to the flesh but according to the Spirit (Rom. 8:1-4)?

Really?

Brian rightly introduced Phinehas into the conversation. Here is the scriptural record:

Then they yoked themselves to the Baal of Peor, and ate sacrifices offered to the dead; they provoked the Lord to anger with their deeds, and a plague broke out among them. Then Phinehas stood up and intervened, and the plague was stayed. And that was counted to him as righteousness from generation to generation forever (Ps. 106:28-31).

Clearly, Phinehas acted, he did something, he accomplished something by his works. And it was 'counted to him as righteousness from generation to generation forever'. Are we to understand this in the sense of '*a clean slate* was counted to him from generation to generation forever'?

David, having spared Saul, declared:

> The Lord rewards every man for his righteousness and his faithfulness, for the Lord gave you into my hand today, and I would not put out my hand against the Lord's anointed (1 Sam. 26:23).

The point is, David was speaking of his works. 'His righteousness' was not merely an absence of sin. He had been positively good in his actions. He had been 'righteous'. And God rewarded him for his works. 'Righteousness' is more than 'a clean slate'.

Of course, we must only apply the old covenant to ourselves in light of the new, yes.[6] And the New Testament shows us how to do it. Clearly, Christ and the apostles did not speak (or write) independently of the old covenant. Far from it. The principles of that covenant were right at the heart of what they were saying! Take for instance, Christ's Sermon on the Mount, particularly Matthew 5. Note, also, the countless references to the law and the prophets in the apostolic writings. The principles set out in the old covenant and its law are fundamental to the New Testament. Consequently, although the old covenant and the Mosaic law are not always overtly referred to, in reading the New Testament we must never forget those principles. The old covenant was a covenant of shadows, yes, but those shadows – law, sabbath, temple (tabernacle), priesthood, sacrifice, altar, and all the rest – were all fulfilled in and by Christ, and their realities belong to every believer through his union with his Redeemer. Christ is the believer's sabbath, priest, sacrifice and so on, and the believer is under the law of Christ. The letter to the Hebrews is replete with this teaching.

What I am saying is, the fact that the righteousness of the old covenant, the righteousness of the law, was a righteousness obtained by works, is essential to a proper understanding of

---

[6] Failure to do this leads to salvation by works. Precisely!

rightcousness in the new covenant. In the old covenant, righteousness was obtained by works, by perfect obedience to the law. That is as plain as a pikestaff:

> What shall we say, then? That Gentiles who did not pursue righteousness have attained it, that is, a righteousness that is by faith; but that Israel who pursued a law that would lead to righteousness did not succeed in reaching that law... the law for righteousness... Moses writes about the righteousness that is based on the law, that the person who does the commandments shall live by them (Rom. 9:30 – 10:5).

The children of Israel were told:

> The Lord commanded us to do all these statutes, to fear the Lord our God, for our good always, that he might preserve us alive, as we are this day. And it will be righteousness for us, if we are careful to do all this commandment before the Lord our God, as he has commanded us (Deut. 6:24-25; see also Deut. 24:13).

So much for the old covenant. Perfect obedience to the law brought righteousness, was righteousness. *The same goes for the new covenant.* With this difference, however: in the old covenant, the righteousness had to be obtained by the works of the individual for himself, whereas in the new covenant, the believer obtains his righteousness vicariously by the work of Christ on his behalf under the law. This is why Christ had to be born sinless under the law (Gal. 4:4). As a man under the law, he had to earn, to merit, deserve, the salvation of his people. The law had to be satisfied, upheld (Matt. 5:17-20; Rom. 3:31). And that is what Christ did. This is what the salvation wrought by the Lord Jesus Christ means. This is what is involved in those familiar passages such as Matthew 1:21; Luke 2:11; John 1:29; Acts 4:12; 5:31; 13:23,38-39; Colossians 1:20-23; 1 Timothy 1:15.

When Job declared: 'I put on righteousness, and it clothed me; my justice was like a robe and a turban' (Job 29:14), as the context makes clear, he was speaking in terms of his works. And he was talking of having more than 'a clean slate'!

And these two following passages must be seen in all their fullness in the new-covenant glory:

Let your priests be clothed with righteousness, and let your saints shout for joy (Ps. 132:9).

I will greatly rejoice in the Lord; my soul shall exult in my God, for he has clothed me with the garments of salvation; he has covered me with the robe of righteousness, as a bridegroom decks himself like a priest with a beautiful headdress, and as a bride adorns herself with her jewels (Isa. 61:10).

They surely go much further than:

Let your priests be clothed with *a clean slate*, and let your saints shout for joy (Ps. 132:9).

I will greatly rejoice in the Lord; my soul shall exult in my God, for he has clothed me with the garments of salvation; he has covered me with the robe of *a clean slate*, as a bridegroom decks himself like a priest with a beautiful headdress, and as a bride adorns herself with her jewels (Isa. 61:10).

This concept of 'clothing' also carries over into the new covenant. See Matthew 22:11; Revelation 3:5; 4:4; 6:11; 7:9,13-14; 19:14.

Take for instance:

For all of you who were [spiritually][7] baptised into Christ have clothed yourselves with Christ (Gal. 3:27, NASB; see also NIV).

And the concept of 'being clothed with' may rightly be extended to that of 'putting on' – as the ESV translates it:

For as many of you as were [spiritually] baptised into Christ have *put on* Christ (Gal. 3:27).

See also:

Put on the Lord Jesus Christ (Rom. 13:15).

Put on the new self, created after the likeness of God in true righteousness and holiness (Eph. 4:24).

Do not lie to one another, seeing that you have put off the old self with its practices and have *put on* the new self, which is being renewed in knowledge after the image of its creator... *Put on* then, as God's chosen ones, holy and beloved... (Col. 3:9-12).

---

[7] See my *Infant*; *Baptist*; *The Hinge*.

Other versions use 'be clothed' or the equivalent in place of 'put on' in those passages.

I am convinced, therefore, that the believer has more than 'a clean slate' imputed to him when he trusts Christ. He is clothed with Christ, he has put on Christ, he has put on the whole Christ. His righteousness in Christ, therefore, also includes perfect obedience to the law – not his own, of course, but his by union with Christ and his perfection.

Was Christ's perfect obedience only a necessary preparation for the cross?

We know that Christ learned obedience by the things that he suffered – suffered throughout his life, and not just on the cross – and that this was an essential part of the lead-up to the cross:

> It was fitting that he, for whom and by whom all things exist, in bringing many sons to glory, should make the founder of their salvation perfect through suffering (Heb. 2:10).

> In the days of his flesh, Jesus offered up prayers and supplications, with loud cries and tears, to him who was able to save him from death, and he was heard because of his reverence. Although he was a son, he learned obedience through what he suffered. And being made perfect, he became the source of eternal salvation to all who obey him, being designated by God a high priest after the order of Melchizedek (Heb. 5:7-10).

> Being found in human form, he humbled himself by becoming obedient to the point of death, even death on a cross (Phil. 2:8).

We all agree that Christ's life leading up to the cross was a life of perfect obedience to the Father under the law (Gal. 4:4), and that this perfection of obedience was essential – to enable him to fulfil the old-covenant requirement and be a perfect, unblemished lamb, to be the Lamb of God (Ex. 12:5; 29:1; Leviticus *passim*; Numbers *passim*; John 1:29,36; 1 Pet. 1:19). The question is: Is that the end of it? Is that all that Christ's perfection of obedience amounts to? Was Christ's perfect obedience under the law a preparatory qualification – an essential qualification, it is true – to enable him to fulfil the old-covenant requirement and be a perfect offering, but, strictly speaking, it has no bearing on the believer?

In the same connection, what about Christ's statement to John the Baptist:

Let it be so now, for thus it is fitting for us to fulfil all righteousness (Matt. 3:15)?

Is there not a reference here to Psalm 40:7-8?[8] How often did Jesus speak of doing his Father's will, obeying his Father, pleasing his Father, and all in connection not only with his work on the cross, but – and especially so – with regard to his life on earth! See John 4:34; 5:36; 8:29; 17:4; 19:28,30. The question is: Is that the end of it? Is that all that Christ's perfection of obedience amounts to? Was it a preparatory qualification – an essential qualification it is true – to enable him to fulfil God's demands under the law, but, strictly speaking, nothing more?

Was Christ's resurrection a vindication of the cross, and therefore a vindication of Christ's accomplishment of justification for his people, and nothing more?

I refer to Geoff's view of Romans 4:25. Here is the verse:

[Christ] was delivered up for our trespasses and raised for our justification (Rom. 4:25).

Paul used *dia* twice: 'delivered up for (*dia*) our trespasses and raised for (*dia*) our justification'. The same weight, surely, must be given in each case. In my view, it is far too weak to say that Christ was raised from the dead simply to vindicate his work, or give proof of the justification he had accomplished for his people on the cross, or to demonstrate that God was being fair to Christ in that since he had earned the pardon, so it was only right that he should be raised. The apostle used *dia*, 'for', 'on account of', in both parts of the sentence. Christ was delivered up *dia* our offences, and was raised *dia* our justification. The apostle clearly attributes the same weight and power to the resurrection as he does to the death of Christ as far as justification goes. Writing to believers, Paul could say that Christ died for our sins, on account of our sins, to deal with our sins, in order to deliver us from our offences, and likewise

---

[8] More of which later.

53

he was raised for our justification, on account of our justification, in order to justify us. This passage, I suggest, on its own, drives a coach and horses through the passive-obedience-only view. 'Vindication' for the second *dia* is woefully inadequate. The truth is, union with Christ is the key to this entire discussion, and union with Christ involves union with him in his death *and* resurrection (Rom. 6:4-8).

Hebrews 10 is critical

This is Geoff's major point. He thinks that the writer's statement in Hebrews 10 is clinching, especially when the context of his (the writer's) immediate quote of Jeremiah 31 is factored in. For Geoff, this passage puts the issue beyond doubt: the cross brings perfection, and perfection is identical to cleansing, 'the forgiveness of sins' – 'the clean slate'. This, of course, takes us back to my first point, which cannot be baulked. If Geoff is right, then justification is forgiveness, and forgiveness is justification; the believer's perfection is a clean slate.

Let me quote the Hebrews passage:

> By a single offering [Christ] has perfected for all time those who are being sanctified. And the Holy Spirit also bears witness to us; for after saying: 'This is the covenant that I will make with them after those days', declares the Lord, 'I will put my laws on their hearts, and write them on their minds', then he adds: 'I will remember their sins and their lawless deeds no more'. Where there is forgiveness of these, there is no longer any offering for sin (Heb. 10:14-18).

Does this passage teach that 'perfection' and 'forgiveness' are one and the same? We know, as Geoff rightly argues, the cross accomplishes perfection for the elect (to be applied to them upon their believing), and this perfection certainly includes forgiveness. But does forgiveness exhaust the perfection? For instance, the believer's new heart, his new mind is also included in Christ's accomplishment, as the above extract shows.

Moreover, within the same context, the writer has just said:

> And by that will we have been sanctified through the offering of the body of Jesus Christ once for all (Heb. 10:10).

So positional sanctification – that is what the writer is referring to in this verse – is also part of the perfection which Christ accomplished on the cross. And positional sanctification is more than 'a clean slate'.[9]

Furthermore, I deliberately retained the opening 'and' in that extract: 'And by that will...'. We need to go back, go back to the start of the chapter:

> For since the law has but a shadow of the good things to come instead of the true form of these realities, it can never, by the same sacrifices that are continually offered every year, make perfect those who draw near. Otherwise, would they not have ceased to be offered, since the worshippers, having once been cleansed, would no longer have any consciousness of sins? But in these sacrifices there is a reminder of sins every year. For it is impossible for the blood of bulls and goats to take away sins. Consequently, when Christ came into the world, he said: 'Sacrifices and offerings you have not desired, but a body have you prepared for me; in burnt offerings and sin offerings you have taken no pleasure. Then I said: "Behold, I have come to do your will, O God, as it is written of me in the scroll of the book"'.
> When he said above: 'You have neither desired nor taken pleasure in sacrifices and offerings and burnt offerings and sin offerings' (these are offered according to the law), then he added: 'Behold, I have come to do your will'. He does away with the first in order to establish the second. And by that will we have been sanctified through the offering of the body of Jesus Christ once for all.
> And every priest stands daily at his service, offering repeatedly the same sacrifices, which can never take away sins. But when Christ had offered for all time a single sacrifice for sins, he sat down at the right hand of God, waiting from that time until his enemies should be made a footstool for his feet. For by a single offering [Christ] has perfected for all time those who are being sanctified. And the Holy Spirit also bears witness to us; for after saying: 'This is the covenant that I will make with them after those days', declares the Lord, 'I will put my laws on their hearts, and write them on their minds', then he adds: 'I will remember their sins and their lawless deeds no more'. Where there is forgiveness of these, there is no longer any offering for sin (Heb. 10:1-18).

---

[9] See my *Fivefold*.

Christ, at his incarnation, addressing his Father,[10] vows to fulfil the will of God, doing so by keeping the law[11] in the body prepared for him by the Father. This, Christ carried out to the full. In his body, from his incarnation (or, at least, his baptism)[12] to the cross and his final *tetelestai* (John 19:30),[13] Christ was always doing the will of God – both in his life and in his death. And in doing that will, in his body Christ wrought something. What? 'And by that will we have been sanctified through the offering of the body of Jesus Christ once for all'; that is, by his obedience to, and fulfilment of, the will of God (including the law of God – see Psalm 40:8), Christ wrought the positional sanctification (Heb. 10:10)[14] to be applied to the elect upon their coming to faith.

In other words, while the one act of Christ's obedience at the cross accomplished the believer's perfection, Christ's entire obedience – in life and death – is what constitutes that perfection and is what is actually imputed to the believer, not merely Christ's work in his dying hours on the cross.[15]

I do not for a moment question that the work was accomplished on the cross:

> As one trespass led to condemnation for all men, so one act of righteousness leads to justification and life for all men. For as by the one man's disobedience the many were made sinners, so by

---

[10] Quoting Ps. 40:7-8.

[11] Do not miss the connection between 'I delight to do your will, O my God; your law is within my heart' (Ps. 40:8) and the promise of the new covenant that God's law would be written on the heart of the believer. Of course, in the new covenant the law of God is the law of Christ, but the point is the law of God permeates both covenants. The law of God for Israel was the law of Moses; the law of God for the believer is the law of Christ. See my *Believers*.

[12] I am not entering that minefield, not having been supplied with a map!

[13] 'It is accomplished'.

[14] Among other things – see, for instance, 1 Cor. 1:30.

[15] I have recently preached two sermons on this theme:
'Christ's Body Prepared: Why?'
(sermonaudio.com/sermoninfo.asp?SID=4917917520)
'Christ's Obedience'
(sermonaudio.com/sermoninfo.asp?SID=5717224112).

the one man's obedience the many will be made righteous (Rom. 5:18-19).

Thus, the question is not: What work of Christ accomplished the believer's perfection? Rather, it is: What does that perfection comprise? I say the cross of Christ accomplishes the perfection, but that perfection includes Christ's active and passive obedience. It is not the body of Christ or the blood of Christ; it is both (John 6:48-58).

So my position is that though the work was done on the cross, the entire obedience of Christ as Mediator is imputed to the believer. As I have said, union with Christ is the key. This is more than representation, as Geoff would have it. Men are either in Adam or in Christ (1 Cor. 15:21-22,45-49; see also Rom. 5:12-19). Men were not constituted sinners in Adam by mere representation. Neither are believers constituted righteous in Christ by mere representation.

What is more, contrary to Geoff's view of Romans 3:31, it is only this perfection by the entire work of the whole Christ – not simply 'a clean state' – that upholds the law, as Paul so confidently asserts that the gospel does (Rom. 3:31).

Finally, while it did not come up in the colloquy (although Geoff got near to it in referring to his covenant-theology background and seminary training), it is often claimed that the active obedience concept is a product of covenant theology. This is not so. It predates covenant theology (which was invented in the 16th century).[16] I do not quote the following to establish my position on this matter, but simply to show that the concept was not invented

---

[16] Although Johann Heinrich Bullinger (1504-1575) was probably the first to publish a work containing the concept, Kaspar Olevianus (1536-1587) was the inventor of covenant theology in Germany, when he and Zacharias Ursinus (1534-1583) drafted the final version of the Heidelberg Catechism (1562). William Ames (1576-1633) was the leading British exponent of covenant theology, which dominated the Westminster Confession of the Presbyterians (1643-1646) and the Savoy Declaration of the Independents (1661). Particular Baptists today, using the 1689 Confession, get as close as they can to covenant theology.

in the 16th or 17th century by covenant theologians. What follows probably dates from the late 2nd century:

> For what else could hide our sins but the righteousness of that one? How could we who were lawless and impious be made upright except by the Son of God alone? Oh the sweet exchange!... That the lawless deeds of many should be hidden by the one who was upright, and the righteousness of one should make upright the many who were lawless![17]

Of course, I suppose it is possible to read it like this:

> For what else could hide our sins but *the clean slate* of that one? How could we who were lawless and impious be made upright (that is, given *a clean slate*) except by the Son of God alone? Oh the sweet exchange!... That the lawless deeds of many should be hidden by the one who was upright (that is, had *a clean slate*), and *the clean slate* of one should make upright (that is, give *a clean slate* to) the many who were lawless!

But I do not think so!

---

[17] Quoted from the 'Epistle of Mathetes (that is, a disciple) to Diognetus'.

Points to Ponder on Christ's Active Obedience

These are just headings, brief points. See my previous articles for detailed arguments.[1]

1. Christ accomplished justification on the cross (Rom. 5:18; Heb. 10:10,14). This is not in dispute. Even so, we must not forget the part played by the resurrection (Rom. 4:25) – taking full account of the double *dia* – nor by Christ's subsequent life (Rom. 5:9-10).

2. The real issue is not the means of the believer's justification, but what precisely is imputed to the believer at the point of faith. The Bible calls this 'righteousness'. The new covenant draws very heavily on the old covenant. What was 'righteousness' in the old covenant? It was obedience to the law: 'It will be righteousness for us, if we are careful to do all this commandment before the Lord our God, as he has commanded us' (Deut. 6:25; see also Deut. 24:13). Righteousness in the old covenant was far more than pardon. It was something positive, something actually done (see Ps. 106:30-31). This principle must not be jettisoned when we come to the new covenant. As Christ is the believer's sabbath, priest, temple, sacrifice, so he is his righteousness. Whatever such things were in shadow in the old covenant, in the new covenant they are the believer's actual experience in Christ.

3. Of course, no man is justified by the works of the law (Gal. 2:16), righteousness does not come by the law (Gal. 2:21), nor could the law impart life, and thus 'righteousness is not based on the law' (Gal. 3:21), but this does not in any way nullify point 2. The fact is, no sinner can keep the law; that is why there is no justification by the law. But, if someone did keep the law,

---

[1] 'Into the Lions' Den: Christ's Active Obedience Re-Visited'; 'Observations on a Colloquy'.

that would be a very different story (Rom. 7:10; 10:5). Christ was born and lived without sin (Acts 3:14; 2 Cor. 5:21; Heb. 4:15; 7:26-27; 1 Pet. 2:22; 1 John 3:5) under the law (Gal. 4:4) to fulfil it (Matt. 5:17), and he did what the law was too weak to accomplish, too weak because man is a sinner (Rom. 8:1-4). And thus Christ, by his obedience to the law in both life and death, laid the basis for Paul's assertion:

Do we then overthrow the law by this faith [that is, by the gospel, especially justification by faith]? By no means! On the contrary, we uphold the law (Rom. 3:31; see Matt. 5:17; Rom. 8:4).

4. 'Righteousness' must be more than 'pardon'. Take this:

One will scarcely die for a righteous person – though perhaps for a good person one would dare even to die – but God shows his love for us in that while we were still sinners, Christ died for us (Rom. 5:7-8).

'Righteous', having 'righteousness', is equivalent to 'good', to being good, not merely 'pardon' or being 'pardoned'. The unconverted are not merely unpardoned sinners. Similarly, saints are not merely pardoned sinners.
As John said:

If you know that he [Christ] is righteous, you may be sure that everyone who practices righteousness has been born of him (1 John 2:29; see John 7:18).

Whoever practices righteousness is righteous, as he [Christ] is righteous (1 John 3:7).

Christ is not 'pardoned', but he is 'righteous', and 'righteousness' is something done.

5. Those who think 'righteousness' means 'pardon' must read the following texts this way:

Unless your *pardon* exceeds that of the scribes and Pharisees, you will never enter the kingdom of heaven (Matt. 5:20).

Gentiles who did not pursue *pardon* have attained it, that is, a *pardon* that is by faith; but... Israel who pursued a law that would lead to *pardon* did not succeed in reaching that law.

Why? Because they did not pursue it by faith, but as if it were based on works... Brothers, my heart's desire and prayer to God for them is that they may be saved. For I bear them witness that they have a zeal for God, but not according to knowledge. For, being ignorant of the *pardon* of God, and seeking to establish their own, they did not submit to God's *pardon*. For Christ is the end of the law for *pardon* to everyone who believes. For Moses writes about the *pardon* that is based on the law, that the person who does the commandments shall live by them. But the *pardon* based on faith says... (Rom. 9:30 – 10:6)

For our sake he [God] made him [Christ] to be sin who knew no sin, so that in him we might become the *pardon* of God (2 Cor. 5:20).

I cannot!

6. Union with Christ is the key. All that Christ, as Mediator, is and all that Christ has done, as Mediator, is the believer's by reason of union with Christ. This must not – cannot – be confined to Christ's work on the cross.

7. If the active obedience of Christ is not imputed to the believer, it means that his obedience to his Father under the law was simply a preparation for the cross, leaving only his work on the cross to be imputed. In which case, at what point precisely did the work of Christ that is imputed to the believer start?

A Theology By Any Other Name...

I am merely musing aloud, you understand, not setting out detailed arguments. They, of course, may be found in my works. Nevertheless, even though what follows consists only of thoughts, I have a purpose – a good, a significant purpose, I believe – in getting my musings down on paper (and out on audio). What I want to do is to stimulate thought and start a conversation.[1]

Some advocates of new-covenant theology have long since had misgivings about the label 'New Covenant Theology'. For my part, at the very least I have a linguistic difficulty with it; new-covenant theology is not a new version of the old covenant-theology which started in the late 16th century. No! Hence my (no doubt, some would say) pedantic use of the hyphen: 'New-Covenant Theology'. Ah well...

Some of us would prefer no label at all, for while labels can be a convenient shortcut, the baggage they usually bring with them can greatly outweigh their benefit. Especially does this apply in theology, where nuances can have a very important role to play. But, it's no use griping over spilt milk; we are, alas, stuck with labels. (No pun intended). And if we advocates of new-covenant theology don't choose one for ourselves, our opponents will readily step into the breach and 'kindly' do it for us – and almost certainly come up with 'Antinomian Theology', or somesuch pejorative term.

It is along these lines that I am thinking aloud. But thinking is allowed is it not?

How about the tag 'Fulfilment Theology'? 'Fulfilment' is a massive New Testament word. It is used far, far more times than the phrase 'new covenant'. It occurs scores and scores of times. And this surely strikes a chord with new-covenant theologians;

---

[1] While this article is not strictly on the subject in hand, it contains relevant material.

we want to be scriptural, do we not? As for frequency of use, when searching for it my *Christ Is All: No Sanctification by the Law*, I admit I was taken aback at the number of times I myself had used the word in that work.

And it is not just its frequency. 'Fulfil' is pregnant with meaning in the New Testament. It is a rich word, very rich indeed.

Christ set the tone right at the start: 'Do not think that I came to destroy the law or the prophets. I did not come to destroy but to fulfil. For assuredly, I say to you, till heaven and earth pass away, one jot or one tittle will by no means pass from the law till all is fulfilled' (Matt. 5:17-18). As Paul said in Galatians 5:14, the Spirit is the 'fulfilment' of the law, its goal, end or aim – which is, to bring about righteousness. The law, though holy, righteous and good (Rom. 7:12), being weak, could not bring about the righteousness that God required. It is the Spirit who has been given to believers in order to effect, to 'fulfil', the law in them, and so establish that righteousness which the law demanded but was unable to produce. Paul was not talking about 'law-works', law-observance, but conformity to Christ (Rom. 8:29), renewal of mind so that the believer can live to God's pleasure (Rom. 12:1-2). This is why Paul, when spelling out the details of the believer's obedience (Rom. 12:1 – 15:13), declares that 'the righteous requirement' of the law is love of neighbour – which 'fulfils' the law (Rom. 13:8). And that touches only the tip of the iceberg. Yes, 'fulfilled' is a massive New Testament word.

Take Matthew's very frequent use of *plēroō* (fulfil) – 16 times. This makes it probable – I would say, certain – that he was thinking in terms of the eschatological. Let me explain. In Matthew 5:17-18, Christ was not abandoning the law, but was bringing out what the law had pointed to. He 'fulfilled' it – the very word he used! Christ was showing continuity with the old covenant, yes, *but also discontinuity*, in the sense of shadow giving way to reality as the new age came in. Moses anticipated Christ, foreshadowed him, but Christ was unique, and so was his teaching. It was new: 'No man ever spoke like this man!' (John 7:46). He alone has the words of eternal life (John 6:68).

There is a further point. Christ said he had not come 'to destroy the law or *the prophets*. I did not come to destroy but to fulfil'. Notice: as with the law, so with the prophets. Just as the prophets (speaking of Christ's first coming) have been fulfilled by Christ, and, therefore, their day is over, so with the law. Consequently, in the same way as we read and use the prophets where Christ has now fulfilled them, so must we read and use the entire law, since he has fulfilled it all. This has an all-important bearing on our understanding of the Old Testament prophecies of 'the law' in the new covenant. Yes, 'fulfilment' is the key.

Of course, in the new covenant, the law and the prophets continue to play an important role in the law of Christ. The law of Christ embraces all Scripture (2 Tim. 3:16-17), including the law (all of it, not just the so-called moral law) and the prophets, but as nuanced by Christ and the apostles. The law and the prophets are 'fulfilled', but, being living Scripture, they still speak today.

Moreover, I am convinced that the concept of 'fulfilment' is vital in the matter of justification. No doubt it is vital in other areas, too, but let me explain what I mean about 'fulfilment' and the cardinal doctrine of justification. We know that when the sinner believes he is united to Christ (Rom. 6:1 – 7:6). The blood of Christ washes him from all sin, from all unrighteousness (1 John 1:9). He is pardoned. But there is more. Righteousness is imputed to him (Rom. 4:11,22-24; Gal. 3:6; Jas. 2:23). And righteousness is more than pardon. This is where 'fulfilment' comes into play. To understand apostolic use of 'righteousness', we must remember that the apostles had been brought up under the old covenant yet now saw the new covenant as fulfilling the old. What was righteousness in the old covenant? It was obedience to God's commandments, his law (Deut. 6:25; Rom. 10:5). Although Israel failed to keep the law, God did not abandon his demand. 'Do and live', he had said (Lev. 18:5; Ezek. 20:11,13; Matt. 19:17; Luke 10:25-28; Rom. 10:5; Gal. 3:12), and that is how it had to be. Perfect obedience would merit life (Rom. 7:10). Alas, no sinner could do the work. But Christ came into the world to save sinners (1 Tim. 1:15), being born under the law (Gal. 4:4), expressly to do his Father's will (Heb. 10:1-18). And this surely included his honouring of the law, his obedience to the law, his fulfilment of the law – both in his life and death. Christ's death and resurrection (Rom 4:25; 5:18-19) secured the justification of the elect, and upon their believing, sinners are perfected forever (Rom. 8:1-4; Heb. 10:10,14), being washed in the blood of Christ, and imputed with his righteousness, he having been imputed with their unrighteousness (2 Cor. 5:21).[2] While not all advocates of new-covenant theology would go along with this,[3] for my part I see the label 'Fulfilment Theology' playing very strongly into this imputation of Christ's righteousness.

Again, 'Fulfilment Theology' reminds us that God's purpose is always fulfilled, that God's way and timing is perfect – even to the very day (Ex. 12:41; 2 Sam. 22:32; Ps. 18:30; Mark 1:15; Gal. 4:4). It also tells us that the progress of God's plan, as seen through his eyes, is always serene. The history of redemption does not consist of God trying one covenant after another, each

---

[2] I admit there is no text which states that Christ's righteousness is imputed to the sinner. But neither is there a text which states that the sinner's unrighteousness is imputed to Christ. Even so, 'the Lord has laid on him the iniquity of us all' (Isa. 53:6) gets pretty close. And sin is imputed to the sinner (Rom. 4:8; 5:13), but not to the believer (Rom. 4:8). As for the exchange between the sinner and Christ – namely, the imputation or transfer of the sinner's unrighteousness to Christ, and Christ's righteousness to the sinner – the law (and before) pictured it admirably (Gen. 22:13; Lev. 1:4; 16:21-22). Christ fulfilled this in reality (Matt. 8:17; Heb. 9:28; 1 Pet. 2:23-25). In other words, Christ bore his people's sin or unrighteousness; they bear his righteousness. See Gal. 2:20; 1 Pet. 3:18. Linking this with Rom. 3:26; 5:10, I am convinced it is right to speak in terms of the great exchange: Christ was imputed with the sin of the elect; the believer is imputed with the righteousness of Christ. And as for no explicit text for it, there is no text which states that justification is on the basis of grace through faith alone. But what evangelical would question that this is the teaching of Scripture?

[3] See my 'Into the Lions' Den: Christ's Active Obedience Re-Visited'; 'Observations on a Colloquy'; 'Points to Ponder on Christ's Active Obedience'.

one ending in a sense of failure. Not at all! Nor are we left to cope with some kind of hybrid of the old and new covenants. No! The old, have fulfilled its purpose, has gone; the new has come. Christ has accomplished it all; he is all (Col. 3:11).

All this would be superbly covered by the label 'Fulfilment Theology'.

So why do I not fall in with it?

The label 'Fulfilment Theology' fails to capture the essential point that we are talking about something that originated with God's decree in eternity, is progressing at his appointed pace and time through history, until in God's purpose all things will be consummated in eternal glory. This is a very powerful principle; it is, perhaps, the most fundamental principle of the lot.[4] We, living in the days of the new covenant, are at this particular stage in God's determined course for the revelation of Christ in all his glory in the salvation of his elect. The days of the old covenant have gone – Christ having fulfilled it and rendered it obsolete (Heb. 8:13), inaugurating the new – but this in itself is only an intermediate stage. Christ will return and usher in the eternal glory (1 Cor. 15:24-28). I suggest that 'Fulfilment Theology' does not sufficiently capture this vital principle. Indeed, it could give the impression that we have reached the end of the road, when we have not! There is more to come (Rom. 8:18-25); work in progress, as it were. Things are not yet 'fulfilled'. We still await the eternal.

So what about 'Progressive-Covenant Theology'; or, to use a term already coined, 'Progressive Covenantalism'? While this is not the zippiest tag in the world – a six-syllable word following one with three syllables is a bit of a mouthful – this certainly has some advantages over 'Fulfilment Theology'. Its stress on the 'progressive' nature of the history of redemption revealed by means of covenants is invaluable. And it certainly implies there is more to come. But, there are for me, at least two serious drawbacks with adopting this label.

---

[4] See my *Redemption*; series of sermons 'Watershed of the Ages'.

'Progressive Covenantalism' is admirably set out in an article by Stephen Wellum and Brent Parker, in which they include the work of Peter Gentry.[5] Now, while there is much that is excellent in their article, much that chimes in with my musings here, I have some serious doubts. Yes, they are clear on the imputation of Christ's active obedience; indeed, they draw particular attention to it. Unfortunately, however, they also want to speak of a pre-fall covenant with all creation. I am not convinced. Moreover, I fear this might leave the door open to the notion of a covenant of works with Adam (and hence all mankind). If so, I would disagree.[6] Furthermore, in my opinion, they leave too much wriggle room for a Jewish kingdom in a millennium after the return of Christ. This introduces a confusion over the land promise: Is this shadow not fulfilled in Christ now, in the new covenant (Col. 2:17), when all the other shadows – sabbath, priest, sacrifice, temple (tabernacle), altar, feast, and so on – are? Once again, Christ is all (Col. 3:11).This confusion over the land promise, I am sure, will lead to difficulties in the future. Further, the idea of a Jewish kingdom raises the spectre of sacrifices being offered yet again, which, if it did rear its head, I would find abhorrent.[7] I do not accuse the originators of the label 'Progressive Covenantalism' of holding these things, but I fear that the troubles I have mentioned might well arise under that label. Consequently I am unwilling to adopt it.

In which case, it seems I am stuck with – if that is the right way of putting it – 'New-Covenant Theology', especially when it includes the hyphen.

As I say, I have just been thinking aloud, and thinking is allowed is it not? May I further remind you that I want to open a conversation? What do you think?

---

[5] Under B&H Academic Blog, see Stephen Wellum and Brent Parker: 'What Is Progressive Covenantalism?' (bhacademicblog.com/what-is-progressive-covenantalism/).
[6] See my 'The Covenant That Never Was'.
[7] See my *Ezekiel*; *Romans 11*.

Sanctification: Jesus and the Believer

Since I have already published extensively on sanctification,[1] I will only say that in this article when I speak of 'sanctification' in connection with Christ, I mean separation or consecration, but when speaking of believers, I go on to include holiness.

Christ is the believer's positional sanctification; the believer is positionally sanctified because he is united to Christ. Take Paul's first letter to the Corinthians, which he addressed to 'the church of God that is in Corinth... those sanctified in Christ Jesus'. The apostle went on to explain:

> Christ Jesus... became to us wisdom from God, righteousness and sanctification and redemption... You were washed, you were sanctified, you were justified in the name of the Lord Jesus Christ and by the Spirit of our God (1 Cor. 1:2,30; 6:11).

And what was true of the Corinthians – the Corinthians, of all people (not the most spiritual of people; see the first letter in full) – is true for every believer throughout this age.

As I say, the believer's sanctification derives explicitly from Christ. Indeed, it derives directly from Christ's own sanctification. As he himself declared, when praying for his people:

> Sanctify them in the truth; your word is truth. As you sent me into the world, so I have sent them into the world. And for their sake I consecrate myself, that they also may be sanctified in truth (John 17:17-19).

Christ made this statement in his great prayer just before his death. It is clear, therefore, that the 'sanctification' he had in mind was his work on the cross. In his prayer, he was sanctifying himself, devoting himself, separating himself to God to go to the cross to shed his blood to redeem his people by his

---

[1] See my *Fivefold*; *Positional*. In addition, see my *Christ*; *Sanctification in Jeremiah*; *Sanctification in Romans*; *Sanctification in Galatians*; *Sanctification in Philippians*.

sacrifice. As a consequence, we can say that the believer is sanctified by Christ's atoning work at Calvary. Indeed, Paul plainly told us so:

> Christ loved the church and gave himself up for her, that he might sanctify her, having cleansed her by the washing of water with the word, so that he might present the church to himself in splendour, without spot or wrinkle or any such thing, that she might be holy and without blemish (Eph. 5:25-27).

> Jesus Christ... gave himself for us to redeem us from all lawlessness and to purify for himself a people for his own possession (Tit. 2:13-14).

And then we have these all-important passages from Hebrews:

> For since the law has but a shadow of the good things to come instead of the true form of these realities, it can never, by the same sacrifices that are continually offered every year, make perfect those who draw near. Otherwise, would they not have ceased to be offered, since the worshippers, having once been cleansed, would no longer have any consciousness of sins? But in these sacrifices there is a reminder of sins every year. For it is impossible for the blood of bulls and goats to take away sins. Consequently, when Christ came into the world, he said: 'Sacrifices and offerings you have not desired, but a body have you prepared for me; in burnt offerings and sin offerings you have taken no pleasure. Then I said: "Behold, I have come to do your will, O God, as it is written of me in the scroll of the book"'.
> When he said above: 'You have neither desired nor taken pleasure in sacrifices and offerings and burnt offerings and sin offerings' (these are offered according to the law), then he added: 'Behold, I have come to do your will'. He does away with the first in order to establish the second. *And by that will we have been sanctified through the offering of the body of Jesus Christ once for all.*
> And every priest stands daily at his service, offering repeatedly the same sacrifices, which can never take away sins. But when Christ had offered for all time a single sacrifice for sins, he sat down at the right hand of God, waiting from that time until his enemies should be made a footstool for his feet. *For by a single offering [Christ] has perfected for all time those who are being*

sanctified.[2] And the Holy Spirit also bears witness to us; for after saying: 'This is the covenant that I will make with them after those days', declares the LORD, 'I will put my laws on their hearts, and write them on their minds', then he adds: 'I will remember their sins and their lawless deeds no more'. Where there is forgiveness of these, there is no longer any offering for sin...
Jesus also suffered outside the gate in order to sanctify the people through his own blood (Heb. 10:1-18; 13:12 see also Heb. 10:29).[3]

So far, so good. Christ, by his work on the cross, sanctified his people. End of story? Far from it! Although Christ did speak of his sanctification – by himself, his own sanctification to the Father – in his great prayer in John 17, and although he was in that prayer referring to his impending death, even so John 17 was not the first time Christ spoke of his sanctification. In John 10, he had already spoken of his sanctification by the Father – the Father's separation of him to the work to which he had been appointed by the Father from eternity past. Christ referred to himself as:

...him whom the Father consecrated [sanctified] and sent into the world (John 10:36).

So it is clear that Christ's sanctification did not begin at the cross. But neither did it begin in John 10! As Christ declared in that passage, he was sanctified by the Father *before his incarnation*. Indeed, Christ's incarnation was a vital aspect of his sanctification by the Father. Christ's sanctification cannot be confined to his work at Calvary. In short, his sanctification originated in God's decree in eternity past, and came into actual and active experience at his incarnation, and went on without a

---

[2] That is, the believer is not only positionally sanctified in Christ, but he inevitably goes on to be progressively sanctified. This is borne out by Heb. 12:14. See my 'Progressive Sanctification: A Matter of Eternal Life or Death'.
[3] At the appropriate time I will explain why I quote this passage in full. But so as to bring out the point I am now making, I have stressed the key words to show that it is by the atoning work of Christ on the cross that the believer is sanctified.

break until and including the cross. All this is part and parcel of his 'sanctification'.

Moreover, the ground had been well and truly prepared, this truth having been laid out in Scripture long before. For a start, Isaiah had repeatedly prophesied the coming of the servant:

> Behold my servant, whom I uphold, my chosen, in whom my soul delights; I have put my Spirit upon him; he will bring forth justice to the nations. He will not cry aloud or lift up his voice, or make it heard in the street; a bruised reed he will not break, and a faintly burning wick he will not quench; he will faithfully bring forth justice. He will not grow faint or be discouraged till he has established justice in the earth; and the coastlands wait for his law (Isa. 42:1-4).

> The LORD called me from the womb, from the body of my mother he named my name... the LORD... formed me from the womb to be his servant (Isa. 49:1).

> The Spirit of the LORD God is upon me, because the LORD has anointed me to bring good news to the poor; he has sent me to bind up the broken-hearted, to proclaim liberty to the captives, and the opening of the prison to those who are bound; to proclaim the year of the LORD's favour, and the day of vengeance of our God; to comfort all who mourn; to grant to those who mourn in Zion – to give them a beautiful headdress instead of ashes, the oil of gladness instead of mourning, the garment of praise instead of a faint spirit; that they may be called oaks of righteousness, the planting of the LORD, that he may be glorified (Isa. 61:1-3).[4]

There is no doubt as to whom these prophecies refer. Christ made it abundantly plain that he himself was their living embodiment:

> [Jesus] came to Nazareth, where he had been brought up. And as was his custom, he went to the synagogue on the sabbath day, and he stood up to read. And the scroll of the prophet Isaiah was given to him. He unrolled the scroll and found the place where it was written: 'The Spirit of the LORD is upon me, because he has anointed me to proclaim good news to the poor. He has sent me to proclaim liberty to the captives and

---

[4] See also Isa. 11:1-10; 48:16.

recovering of sight to the blind, to set at liberty those who are oppressed, to proclaim the year of the LORD's favour'. And he rolled up the scroll and gave it back to the attendant and sat down. And the eyes of all in the synagogue were fixed on him. And he began to say to them: 'Today this Scripture has been fulfilled in your hearing' (Luke 4:16-21).[5]

Clearly, before his incarnation Christ had been set apart as the Father's Servant, sanctified to the work appointed for him.

Then we have the glorious statement at the opening of Hebrews – that momentous book on the glories of the new covenant, and its superiority over the old:

Long ago, at many times and in many ways, God spoke to our fathers by the prophets, but in these last days he has spoken to us by his Son, whom he appointed the heir of all things, through whom also he created the world. He is the radiance of the glory of God and the exact imprint of his nature, and he upholds the universe by the word of his power. After making purification for sins, he sat down at the right hand of the Majesty on high, having become as much superior to angels as the name he has inherited is more excellent than theirs. For to which of the angels did God ever say: 'You are my Son, today I have begotten you'? Or again: 'I will be to him a father, and he shall be to me a son'? And again, when he brings the firstborn into the world, he says: 'Let all God's angels worship him'. Of the angels he says: 'He makes his angels winds, and his ministers a flame of fire'. But of the Son he says: 'Your throne, O God, is forever and ever, the sceptre of uprightness is the sceptre of your kingdom. You have loved righteousness and hated wickedness; therefore God, your God, has anointed you with the oil of gladness beyond your companions'. And: 'You, Lord, laid the foundation of the earth in the beginning, and the heavens are the work of your hands; they will perish, but you remain; they will all wear out like a garment, like a robe you will roll them up, like a garment they will be changed. But you are the same, and your years will have no end' (Heb. 1:1-12).[6]

Once again the point is made: the Father had appointed Christ to his work, sanctified him, long before his incarnation.

---

[5] See also Isa. 35 with Matt. 11:5; Luke 7:22.
[6] See my series of sermons 'Watershed of the Ages'.

What God said to Jeremiah could also be said of Christ, but with a much greater significance:

> Before I formed you in the womb I knew you, and before you were born I consecrated you; I appointed you a prophet to the nations (Jer. 1:5).

In Christ's case, he was the fulfilment of Moses' prophecy:

> The LORD your God will raise up for you a prophet like me from among you, from your brothers – it is to him you shall listen... I will raise up for them a prophet like you from among their brothers. And I will put my words in his mouth, and he shall speak to them all that I command him. And whoever will not listen to my words that he shall speak in my name, I myself will require it of him (Deut. 18:15-19).

And then we have the episode with Simeon in the temple:

> There was a man in Jerusalem, whose name was Simeon, and this man was righteous and devout, waiting for the consolation of Israel, and the Holy Spirit was upon him. And it had been revealed to him by the Holy Spirit that he would not see death before he had seen the LORD's Christ. And he came in the Spirit into the temple, and when the parents brought in the child Jesus, to do for him according to the custom of the law, he took him up in his arms and blessed God and said: 'LORD, now you are letting your servant depart in peace, according to your word; for my eyes have seen your salvation that you have prepared in the presence of all peoples, a light for revelation to the Gentiles, and for glory to your people Israel'. And his father and his mother marvelled at what was said about him. And Simeon blessed them and said to Mary his mother: 'Behold, this child is appointed for the fall and rising of many in Israel, and for a sign that is opposed (and a sword will pierce through your own soul also), so that thoughts from many hearts may be revealed' (Luke 2:25-34).

Anna, too, joined in and 'began to give thanks to God and to speak of [Jesus] to all who were waiting for the redemption of Jerusalem' (Luke 2:38).[7]

---

[7] See my series of sermons 'Watershed of the Ages'. See also Matt. 21:11; Luke 7:16; 24:19; John 1:21,25; 4:19; Acts 7:37.

Of John the Baptist it was said:

He will be filled with the Holy Spirit, even from his mother's womb (Luke 1:15).

John was filled with the Spirit from his mother's womb, filled with the Spirit to do the work to which had been appointed by God. In other words, John was 'sanctified' from the womb. How much more so in the case of Christ.

And Paul could speak of it for himself:

He who had set me apart before I was born, and who called me by his grace, was pleased to reveal his Son to me, in order that I might preach him among the Gentiles (Gal. 1:15-16).

In other words, Paul had been 'set apart' – sanctified, in this sense – to his life's work. As the Lord said to him:

I am Jesus whom you are persecuting. But rise and stand upon your feet, for I have appeared to you for this purpose, to appoint you as a servant and witness to the things in which you have seen me and to those in which I will appear to you, delivering you from your people and from the Gentiles – to whom I am sending you to open their eyes, so that they may turn from darkness to light and from the power of Satan to God, that they may receive forgiveness of sins and a place among those who are sanctified by faith in me (Acts 26:15-18).

All this was true of Christ himself: he had been appointed – sanctified – by the Father to his great work as Mediator.

In a general – but far lesser – sense, every child of God can say this sort of thing:

My frame was not hidden from you, when I was being made in secret, intricately woven in the depths of the earth. Your eyes saw my unformed substance; in your book were written, every one of them, the days that were formed for me, when as yet there was none of them (Ps. 139:15-16).

Yes, but all this is true of Christ in the highest possible sense of the words. Christ had been sanctified by the Father from eternity past.

Let me underline this. Christ's sanctification – the sanctification we are talking about in connection with the

75

believer – did not begin at the cross. It began in eternity; more especially, it came into effect in his incarnation in Mary's womb. Consequently, we may with confidence say that Christ was sanctified by the Father in the manger, sanctified in the carpenter's shop, sanctified in his baptism, sanctified in his itinerant preaching, sanctified in his miracle working, all this culminating in his sanctification to the work the Father had for him to do on the cross. Throughout his life he was always the Holy One of God, always dedicated or sanctified to his Father's work. As he said as a lad in the temple: 'Did you not know that I must be in my Father's house?' Or: 'Did you not know that I must be about my Father's business?' (Luke 2:49). There never was a time when Christ was not doing his 'Father's business'.[8]

This is the very point that had been revealed to Peter. How clearly we see this in his reply to Christ, who had challenged his disciples about joining the crowd and forsaking him:

Lord, to whom shall we go? You have the words of eternal life, and *we have believed, and have come to know, that you are the Holy One of God* (John 6:68-69).[9]

And we have this:

Now when Jesus came into the district of Caesarea Philippi, he asked his disciples: 'Who do people say that the Son of Man is?' And they said: 'Some say John the Baptist, others say Elijah, and others Jeremiah or one of the prophets'. He said to them: 'But who do you say that I am?' Simon Peter replied: 'You are the Christ, the Son of the living God'. And Jesus answered him: 'Blessed are you, Simon Bar-Jonah! For flesh and blood has not revealed this to you, but my Father who is in heaven (Matt. 16:13-17).

Peter put the matter beyond doubt when he told the Jews of:

...Jesus, whom heaven must receive until the time for restoring all the things about which God spoke by the mouth of his holy prophets long ago. Moses said: 'The LORD God will raise up for you a prophet like me from your brothers. You shall listen

---

[8] See also John 4:34; 5:36, which I will quote below.
[9] See also Mark 1:24; Luke 1:35; 4:34; Acts 3:14.

to him in whatever he tells you. And it shall be that every soul who does not listen to that prophet shall be destroyed from the people' (Acts 3:20-23).

Nor must we forget that all this had been securely rooted in the principles of the old covenant given to Israel through Moses at Sinai, clearly set out (for those with eyes to see) in Scripture in the law and prophets. I have already referred to Deuteronomy, and to Isaiah and his extensive prophecies. As Christ told the disciples on the road to Emmaus:

'O foolish ones, and slow of heart to believe all that the prophets have spoken! Was it not necessary that the Christ should suffer these things and enter into his glory?' And beginning with Moses and all the prophets, he interpreted to them in all the Scriptures the things concerning himself (Luke 24:25-27).

Later that same evening, addressing the fearful disciples gathered in secret in Jerusalem, Christ declared:

'These are my words that I spoke to you while I was still with you, that everything written about me in the law of Moses and the prophets and the psalms must be fulfilled'. Then he opened their minds to understand the Scriptures (Luke 24:44-45).

The point needs to be broadened. To state the obvious (but, alas, not always remembered) fact, the New Testament did not start from scratch. God, from the beginning of time, had been revealing his master-plan of redemption, revealing it in history through a series of covenants, unveiling it progressively from stage to stage according to his eternal decree, bringing each stage to its appointed end or fulfilment. As soon as man fell, God had issued his glorious promise of redemption. In cursing Satan, in ringing tones God had set out his promise to send the Redeemer to accomplish redemption for his people. Addressing the serpent, God solemnly but triumphantly declared:

I will put enmity between you and the woman, and between your offspring and her offspring; he shall bruise your head, and you shall bruise his heel (Gen. 3:15).

And throughout the rest of the Old Testament, God progressively set this out again and again in types and shadows, increasingly revealing to men the glorious work that the sanctified Redeemer would come and do for his people. Take Abraham with Isaac on Moriah. When Isaac questioned his father concerning the sacrifice they were about to offer:

Abraham said: 'God will provide for himself the lamb for a burnt offering, my son'.

And this led to the glorious culmination that day:

Abraham lifted up his eyes and looked, and behold, behind him was a ram, caught in a thicket by his horns. And Abraham went and took the ram and offered it up as a burnt offering instead of his son. So Abraham called the name of that place: 'The LORD will provide' (Gen. 22:8,13-14).

Nowhere was all this more fully set out than in the covenant God gave to Israel through Moses at Sinai. Of the scores and scores of illustrations to make the point, consider the way the old covenant typified or foreshowed this concept of Christ's consecration to the priesthood, his separation to the work decreed for him by the Father:

You... shall anoint them [Aaron your brother... his sons with him] and ordain them and consecrate them, that they may serve me as priests... This is what you shall do to them to consecrate them, that they may serve me as priests... (Ex. 28:41; 29:1).

Moses took some of the anointing oil and of the blood that was on the altar and sprinkled it on Aaron and his garments, and also on his sons and his sons' garments. So he consecrated Aaron and his garments, and his sons and his sons' garments with him (Lev. 8:30).

And so on, and on.

We must never forget that the Old Testament (the old covenant, in particular) permeates the New Testament (the new covenant). We shall never fully understand the latter unless this fundamental fact is taken into account. Take the Sermon on the Mount. Whatever else may be said about that discourse, it depends absolutely on the old covenant.

Coming closer to the issue in hand, consider 'righteousness' in Romans. I raise this because, when thinking about the believer, righteousness and sanctification are intimately linked. 'Righteousness' (with its family members) appears scores of times in Romans. Trying to come to an understanding of Paul's use of 'righteousness' in Romans, without bearing in mind the principles of the old covenant, is bound to lead to disaster. The number of references to the Old Testament throughout the book, on its own, is enough to knock that scheme on the head. Moreover, the apostle's detailed arguments based on the Old Testament – see Romans 3, 4, 9 and 10, for instance, but throughout the book – put the point beyond doubt. Coming at it from the other direction, when reading Romans, it is essential to wear the same spectacles (or hearing aid) as the first readers (hearers) of the letter. What did the believers at Rome hear when Paul's letter was read to them? What did they bring to what was being said? What were their presuppositions? There is no doubt as to the answers to those questions. Paul could say with confidence: 'I am speaking to those who know the law' (Rom. 7:1).[10] Working on that fact, he could develop his argument – as he did (Rom. 7:1-6) – assured in the knowledge that his readers would be following him all the way.

And that is how we must read Romans (or any other portion of Scripture). We forget this elementary principle at our peril.[11] And as for 'righteousness' in this regard, see Romans 9:30 – 10:5.[12] This passage, on its own, tells us what Paul meant by 'righteousness' in Romans. Paul was certainly not limiting 'righteousness' to pardon! God's revealed mind in the old covenant – the principle, God's demand, being carried over into the new – would never allow that! God is unchanging and unchangeable: 'I the LORD do not change' (Mal. 3:6; see Rom.

---

[10] For more on this point, see my *Christ*.
[11] See my 'Asking the Wrong Question'.
[12] See my *Peter Masters' Muddle*.

11:29). He demanded perfection in the old covenant; he obtained it in Christ in the new.[13]

Pulling all this together, we see that God's eternal decree separated Christ ('Christ' means 'anointed') to his life-long work as Mediator. As Peter told Cornelius and the crowd that had gathered in his home:

> God anointed Jesus of Nazareth with the Holy Spirit and with power. He went about doing good and healing all who were oppressed by the devil, for God was with him. And we are witnesses of all that he did both in the country of the Jews and in Jerusalem. They put him to death by hanging him on a tree, but God raised him on the third day and made him to appear, not to all the people but to us who had been chosen by God as witnesses, who ate and drank with him after he rose from the dead. And he commanded us to preach to the people and to testify that he is the one appointed by God to be judge of the living and the dead. To him all the prophets bear witness that everyone who believes in him receives forgiveness of sins through his name (Acts 10:38-43; see also Isa. 32:1; 61:1; Dan. 9:25-26; Matt. 26:6-13; Luke 7:37-50, and so on).

God foreshadowed this through the history of redemption set out in a series of covenants – specially the Abrahamic, Mosaic and Davidic.[14] In the fullness of time (Gal. 4:4), God sent his Son into the world born of a woman under the law in order to fulfil it (Matt. 5:17-18; Heb. 8:13). God sent his Son! Do not miss the way in which John stressed this very point:

> For God so loved the world, that he gave his only Son, that whoever believes in him should not perish but have eternal life. For God did not send his Son into the world to condemn the world, but in order that the world might be saved through him (John 3:16-17).

---

[13] See my 'Into the Lions' Den: Christ's Active Obedience Re-Visited'; 'Observations on a Colloquy'; 'Points to Ponder on Christ's Active Obedience'; 'Asking the Wrong Question'.

[14] See my *Redemption*.

On him [that is, Christ] God the Father has set his seal... This is the work of God, that you believe in him whom he has sent... The living Father sent me (John 6:27-29,57).

I have not come of my own accord. He who sent me is true, and him you do not know. I know him, for I come from him, and he sent me (John 7:28-29).

I came from God and I am here. I came not of my own accord, but he sent me (John 8:42).

...him whom the Father consecrated and sent into the world (John 10:36).

Jesus lifted up his eyes and said: 'Father, I thank you that you have heard me. I knew that you always hear me, but I said this on account of the people standing around, that they may believe that you sent me' (John 11:41-42).

This is eternal life, that they know you, the only true God, and Jesus Christ whom you have sent. I glorified you on earth, having accomplished the work that you gave me to do. And now, Father, glorify me in your own presence with the glory that I had with you before the world existed. I have manifested your name to the people whom you gave me out of the world. Yours they were, and you gave them to me, and they have kept your word. Now they know that everything that you have given me is from you. For I have given them the words that you gave me, and they have received them and have come to know in truth that I came from you; and they have believed that you sent me... As you sent me into the world, so I have sent them into the world. And for their sake I consecrate myself, that they also may be sanctified in truth. I do not ask for these only, but also for those who will believe in me through their word, that they may all be one, just as you, Father, are in me, and I in you, that they also may be in us, so that the world may believe that you have sent me... O righteous Father, even though the world does not know you, I know you, and these know that you have sent me (John 17:3-8,18-21,25).

As the Father has sent me, even so I am sending you (John 20:21).[15]

---

[15] This list does not exhaust the point in John's Gospel – see below.

In this the love of God was made manifest among us, that God sent his only Son into the world, so that we might live through him. In this is love, not that we have loved God but that he loved us and sent his Son to be the propitiation for our sins... And we have seen and testify that the Father has sent his Son to be the Saviour of the world (1 John 4:9-14).

So Christ's sanctification – which, I remind you, leads directly to the believer's sanctification – must not be confined to the cross. Right from his incarnation, Christ's entire life was spent doing the will of God. Take one example. Christ's baptism. The Lord's response to John's unwillingness to baptise him was no makeweight; it set the tone for his entire life and ministry:

Let it be so now, for thus it is fitting for us to fulfil all righteousness (Matt. 3:15).

And what Paul declared of David (who was a dim foreshadow of Christ – see Ps. 2:6; Is. 11:10; Matt. 2:2; 27:11,29,37; Luke 1:32; John 12:15; 19:19; Acts 2:30; Rom. 11:26; Rev. 5:5; 22:16), could well be said of Christ:

[God] raised up David to be their [Israel's] king, of whom he testified and said: 'I have found in David the son of Jesse a man after my heart, who will do all my will' (Acts 13:22; see 1 Sam. 15:22; Acts 7:46).

The point is, Saul had been rejected because he had not kept God's commandment, whereas David would. As God could declare to Saul:

Your kingdom shall not continue. The LORD has sought out a man after his own heart, and the LORD has commanded him to be prince over his people, because you have not kept what the LORD commanded you (1 Sam. 13:14).

And David's words in Psalm 18 are surely Messianic:

The LORD dealt with me according to my righteousness; according to the cleanness of my hands he rewarded me. For I have kept the ways of the LORD, and have not wickedly departed from my God. For all his rules [just decrees] were before me, and his statutes I did not put away from me. I was blameless before him, and I kept myself from my guilt. So the

LORD has rewarded me according to my righteousness, according to the cleanness of my hands in his sight (Ps. 18:20-24).

And this is precisely why I quoted Hebrews 10:1-18 in full. Yes, the cross is the climax of that passage, but it is the culmination of a section of massive significance setting out Christ's obedience to the Father's will and commandment throughout his entire life on earth. This life-long sanctification of Christ must not be brushed aside as a mere preparation for the cross.[16]

As Christ said, time and again throughout his life on earth (and he was not confining his remarks to the cross, please note):

My food is to do the will of him who sent me and to accomplish his work (John 4:34).

I can do nothing on my own. As I hear, I judge, and my judgment is just, because I seek not my own will but the will of him who sent me...The testimony that I have is greater than that of John [the Baptist]. For the works that the Father has given me to accomplish, the very works that I am doing, bear witness about me that the Father has sent me. And the Father who sent me has himself borne witness about me (John 5:30,36-37).

I have come down from heaven, not to do my own will but the will of him who sent me. And this is the will of him who sent me, that I should lose nothing of all that he has given me, but raise it up on the last day. For this is the will of my Father, that everyone who looks on the Son and believes in him should have eternal life, and I will raise him up on the last day (John 6:38-40).

He who sent me is with me. He has not left me alone, for I always do the things that are pleasing to him (John 8:29).

Addressing his Father, Christ declared:

I glorified you on earth, having accomplished the work that you gave me to do (John 17:4).

Jesus, knowing that all was now finished... he said: 'It is finished' (John 19:28-30).

---

[16] See my 'Observations on a Colloquy'.

So where is this going? What is my concern in going into all this? It all points to one conclusion. Which is? The entire life of Christ plays a vital part in his work of redemption for his people. Yes, Christ on the cross accomplished redemption, but Christ's life, his doing of his Father's will, his completing the work he had been given, culminating in his glorious *tetelestai* – 'It is finished' (John 19:30) – all this is the fulfilment of the old covenant's foreshadowing of his separation or consecration to his Father's will. Christ was sanctified by the Father; Christ sanctified himself; and all that he might sanctify his people. And all is fulfilled in Christ's complete life from the moment of his incarnation. His active obedience before the cross was not just a preparation for the cross. Rather, that entire obedience was an integral part of his sanctification which is imputed to the sinner as he trusts Christ for salvation. In his believing, the sinner is united to Christ, and receives the imputation of Christ's perfect sanctification, so that he himself is immediately positionally sanctified in Christ, perfected for ever (Heb. 10:10,14).

In short, it is not simply what is known as the passive obedience of Christ (his death) that is imputed to the believing sinner. No! Imputed righteousness and sanctification comes from the whole Christ, his entire, life-long, obedience to the Father in his sanctification from eternity as Mediator, culminating in his death and resurrection. This was Christ's sanctification. And it is every believer's sanctification.

Comments by others

First, the general point.

John Calvin in his *Institutes*:

> Christ was sanctified from earliest infancy, that he might sanctify his elect in himself... For as he, in order to wipe away the guilt of disobedience which had been committed in our flesh, assumed that very flesh, that in it he might, on our account, and in our stead, perform a perfect obedience, so he was conceived by the Holy Spirit, that, completely pervaded

with his holiness in the flesh which he had assumed, he might transfuse[17] it into us.

Then John 17:19, taking it as Christ's sanctification in the sense of his work on the cross.

Charles J.Ellicott:

> The consecration here thought of is that to the work which was immediately before [Christ] – the offering [of] himself as a sacrifice. The word was in frequent use in the special sense of an offering or sacrifice set apart to God. As a New Testament example of this, compare Romans 15:16. By this consecration of himself... he will, as both priest and sacrifice, enter into the Holy of Holies of the heavenly temple, and will send the Holy Ghost, who will consecrate [those for whom he was praying].

Matthew Poole:

> I sanctify myself, here, is no more than, I set myself apart, as a sacrifice acceptable and well pleasing in the sight of God: and

---

[17] I allow the word to stand. 'Transfuse' can mean 'transfer' or 'transmit'. In other words, Calvin might have been speaking of imputed or imparted holiness. Both are scriptural. Here, by his use of 'into', I take it that he meant 'imparted'. Rome confuses the two, but Scripture is clear. 'What the law could not do in that it was weak through the flesh, God did by sending his own Son... that the righteous requirement of the law might be fulfilled in us' (Rom. 8:3-4); that is, believers. Echoes here of Gal. 4:4-5. By Christ's work, "the righteous requirement of the law" is "fulfilled in us". "Fulfilled", "fulfilled in us"! Clearly, this is something which God in Christ has done *for* and *in* believers, not something to be done *by* believers trying to keep the law. Paul here *describes* believers; he does not tell them to fulfil the law. God, by his Son, Christ Jesus, accomplished the fulfilment of the righteous requirement of the law, and it is this perfect obedience of Christ, his righteousness, which is imputed and imparted to believers. Thus Christ fulfilled the law, and believers have fulfilled it in him. Christ's work imputed to them by the Spirit accomplishes their justification [and positional sanctification]. Christ's work imparted to them by the Spirit accomplishes their [progressive] sanctification. And it is this [progressive] sanctification which is the evidence and fruit of the fulfilment of the righteous requirement of the law in believers in and by Christ' (quoted from my *Christ* pp174-175).

indeed sanctifying, in the ancient notion of it under the law, did ordinarily signify the setting of persons and things apart to the special service of God; which was done legally by certain ritual performances and ceremonies, and is still done inwardly and spiritually by regeneration, and renewing of the hearts of men and women by the efficacious working of the Holy Ghost. Christ says that for his disciples' sake he sanctified himself, being both the priest and the sacrifice. Christ set apart himself as a sacrifice for his people.

John Gill:

This may be meant of his [Christ's] being separated, and set apart for his office as Mediator, which, though done by the Father, and is ascribed unto him (John 10:36), yet may also be attributed to himself, since he voluntarily devoted himself to this work, and cheerfully accepted of it: though it seems best to understand it of his offering himself a sacrifice for, and in the room and stead of his people, in allusion to the offerings under the law, the sacrificing of which is expressed by sanctifying (Ex. 13:2); and because his sacrifice was an holy one, what he sanctified or offered was himself... his body and his soul; and these as in union with his divine person; which gives his sacrifice the preference to all others, and is the true reason of its virtue and efficacy; and this is expressive of his great love. He himself is also the sanctifier or offerer, which shows him to be a priest, and that he had a power over his own life, and that he sacrificed it voluntarily; and this he is said to do at that present time, because the time was very near that he was to be offered up, and his present prayer and intercession were a part of his priestly office.

Take John 10:36, Christ's sanctification speaking of more than his work on the cross.

John Calvin:

This refers strictly to the person of Christ, so far as he is manifested in the flesh. Accordingly, these two things are joined, that he has been sanctified and sent into the world.

In his *Institutes*, Calvin (alas, too gently) drew attention to a vital distinction about the 'righteousness' that is imputed to the believer; namely, that it is Christ's life-long obedience under the law, not his intrinsic righteousness:

Although righteousness comes to us from the secret fountain of the Godhead, it does not follow that Christ, who sanctified himself in the flesh on our account, is our righteousness in respect of his divine nature (John 17:19).

Charles J.Ellicott:

The tense refers to the time of [Christ's] consecration to his Messianic work, and to the incarnation, which was the commencement of it.

John Gill:

Sanctification here designs... and respects the eternal separation of [Christ] to his office, as Mediator, in the counsel, purposes, and decrees of God... being pre-ordained thereunto before the foundation of the world... and sent into the world in human nature, to obtain eternal redemption and [the] salvation [of] his people: to save them from sin, Satan, the world, law, hell and death, which none but God could do.

Albert Barnes:

God has consecrated or appointed his Son to be his Messenger or Messiah to mankind.

M.R.Vincent:

Consecrated. The fundamental idea of the word is separation and consecration to the service of Deity.

John Trapp:

Sanctified, that is, anointed, and that in both his natures, as whole Christ. For his anointing imported, 1. His consecration or ordination to the office of a Mediator, and so the Godhead also was anointed. 2. Qualification or effusion of fullness of graces; as the holy oil was compounded of [various] spices, so the manhood, and that without measure, as far as a finite nature was capable of.

C.H.Spurgeon on Hebrews 10:10:

We shall, *first*, speak of the eternal will. *Secondly* of the effectual sacrifice by which that will has been carried out. And *thirdly*, of the everlasting result accomplished by that will through the sacrifice of the body of Christ. May the Holy Spirit who has revealed the grand doctrine of justification now enable us to understand it and to feel its comforting power.

First, then, the eternal will – 'By the which will we are sanctified'. This will must, first of all, be viewed as the will ordained of old by the Father – the eternal decree of the infinite Jehovah that a people whom he chose should be sanctified and set apart unto himself...

His will is the Alpha and the Omega of all things. It was according to this eternal, invincible will of God that he chose, created, and set apart a people that should show forth the glory and riches of his grace – a people that would bear the image of his only-begotten Son, a people that should joyfully and willingly serve him in his courts forever and ever – a people who should be his own sons and daughters, to whom he would say: 'I will dwell in them and walk in them and they shall be my people and I will be their God'. Thus stood the eternal will of old. 'For whom he did foreknow, he also did predestinate to be conformed to the image of his Son, that he might be the firstborn among many brethren'.

But, of course, by nature the elect are dead in sins, utterly polluted:

> But the people concerning whom this will was made were dead in sin, defiled with evil, polluted by transgression. The old serpent's venom was in their veins. They were fit to be set apart for the curse, but not to be set apart for the service of the thrice holy God. And the question was, how then should the will of the Immutable Invincible ever be carried out? How shall these rebels become absolved? How shall these fountains of filth become clear as crystal, pouring forth floods of living water and divine praise? How shall these unsanctified and defiled ones become sanctified unto the service of God? It must be – but how shall it be?

Spurgeon turned to the old covenant, the priests and the sacrifices. But the Mosaic covenant, though instituted by God, provided no effectual salvation, never effectively sanctified any sinner:

[God's] will was not fulfilled in them. It was not his will that they [that is, the old-covenant priests and their sacrifices] should sanctify the people. They were inefficacious to such an end for, as the Holy Spirit has said, it was 'not possible that the blood of bulls and of goats should take away sins'. And so, if these offerings had been all, centuries of the house of Aaron and of the priests of the tribe of Levi might have come and gone, and yet the will decreed by the eternal Father would not have been an accomplished fact.

Even so, God had always planned it thus; he always planned to sanctify – separate – his Son, and send him into the world, under the old covenant, in order to fulfil it and render perfect obedience to the law, and so establish the new, superior, better, effective covenant in Christ.

Spurgeon:

> Thus we are landed at our *second* point, which is, that this will by which we are sanctified was performed by the ever-blessed Son. It was the will of God the Father, but it was carried out by the divine Son when he came into the world. A body was prepared for him and into that body, in a mysterious manner which we will not attempt even to conceive of, he entered and there he was – the incarnate God. This incarnate God, by offering his own blood, by laying down his own life, by bearing in his own body the curse, and in his own spirit enduring the wrath was able to effect the purpose of the everlasting Father in the purging of his people, in the setting of his chosen apart, and making them henceforth holiness unto the LORD. Do you not see what the will of the Father was – that he should have a people that should be sanctified unto himself? But that will could not be carried out by the blood of bulls and of goats. It must be achieved by the offering up of the body of Jesus Christ once for all. Our Lord Jesus Christ has done whatever that will of the Father required for its perfect achievement. This is our satisfaction.

Spurgeon spoke of the essential work of the Spirit in applying Christ's work:

> Thus it is by the will of the Father, carried out by the Son, and applied by the Holy Spirit that the church of God is regarded as sanctified before God and is acceptable unto him.

Spurgeon then addressed:

> ...the effectual sacrifice of Christ by which the will of God with regard to the sanctity of his people has been carried out: 'By the which will we are sanctified through the offering of the body of Jesus Christ'.

Spurgeon:

> This implies, first, his incarnation, which of course includes his eternal deity... The gospel of his incarnation is not a spiritual idea, nor a metaphor, nor a myth. In very deed and truth, the God that made heaven and earth came down to earth and hung upon a woman's breast as an infant. That child, as he grew in stature and wisdom, was as certainly God as he is at this moment in glory. He was as surely God when he was here hungry and suffering, sleeping, eating, drinking as he was God when he hung up the morning stars and kindled the lamps of night, or as he shall be when sun and moon shall dim at the brightness of his coming. Jesus Christ, very God of very God, did certainly stoop to become such as we are and was made in the likeness of sinful flesh. It is a truth you all know, but I want you to grasp it and realise it. It will help you to trust Christ if you clearly perceive that, divine as he is, he is bone of your bone and flesh of your flesh – your kinsman, though the Son of God.

Spurgeon tackled a vital nuance in all this:

> All this is implied in the text, because it speaks of the offering of the body of Christ. But why does it specially speak of the body? I think [it is] to show us the reality of that offering – his soul suffered and his soul's sufferings were the soul of his sufferings, but still, to make it palpable to us, to record it as a sure historical fact, the Holy Spirit mentions that there was an offering of the body of Christ.

But this is not all. And here Spurgeon came close to the point I have been trying to make in this article:

> I take it, however, that the word means the whole of Christ – that there was an offering made of all of Christ, the body of him or that of which he was constituted... I look upon our Lord Jesus as in his very Godhead stooping down to bear the weight of human sin and human misery, sustaining it because he was

divine and able to bear what else had been too great a load. Thus the whole of Christ was made a sacrifice for sin. It was the offering, not of the spirit of Christ, but of the very body of Christ – the essence, subsistence, and most manifest reality and personality of Jesus Christ, the Son of the Most High.

He probed deeper:

And this was wholly offered. I do not know how to bring out my own thoughts here, but to accomplish the will of God in sanctifying all his people, Christ must be the offering and he must be wholly offered... as our sin-offering, making expiation for guilt, our blessed Lord and Master gave himself wholly for us as an atoning sacrifice and offering for sin – and that 'himself', sums up all you can conceive it to be in and of the Christ of God, and the pangs and griefs which, like a fire went through him, did consume him, even to the uttermost of all that was in him. He bore all that could be borne, stooped to the lowest to which humility could come, descended to the utmost abyss to which a descent of self-denial could be made. He made himself of no reputation. He emptied himself of all honour and glory. He gave up himself without reserve. He saved others, himself he could not save – he spares us in our chastisements, but himself he spared not. He says of himself in the twenty-second psalm: 'I am a worm and no man; a reproach of men and despised of the people'. You do not know, you cannot imagine how fully the sacrifice was made by Christ. It was not only a sacrifice of all of himself, but a complete sacrifice of every part of himself for us. The blaze of eternal wrath for human sin was focused upon his head! The anguish that must have been endured by him who stood in the place of millions of sinners to be judged of God and smitten in their stead is altogether inconceivable. Though himself perfectly innocent, yet in his own person to offer up such a sacrifice as could honour the divine justice on account of myriads of sins of myriads of the sons of men was a work far beyond all human realisation. You may give loose to your reason and your imagination and rise into the seventh heaven of sublime conception as with eagle wing, but you can never reach the utmost height. Here is the sum of the matter – 'Thanks be unto God for his unspeakable gift', for unspeakable, inconceivable it certainly is when we view the Lord Jesus as a sacrifice for the sins of men...

Spurgeon, having spoken of expiation and reconciliation, moved on:

> Moreover, they [that is, believers] are not only accepted and reconciled, but they are purified – the taint that was upon them is taken away. In God's sight they are regarded no more as unclean. They are no longer shut outside the camp – they may come to the throne of the heavenly grace whenever they will. God can have communion with them. He regards them as fit to stand in his courts and to be his servants, for they are purified, reconciled, expiated through the one offering of Christ. Their admission into the closest intimacy with God could never be allowed if he did not regard them as purged from all uncleanness and this has been effected not at all by themselves, but only by the great sacrifice:

> *Your blood, not mine, O Christ,*
> *Your blood so freely spilt,*
> *Has blanched my blackest stains,*
> *And purged away my guilt.*
> *Your righteousness, O Christ,*
> *Alone does cover me.*
> *No righteousness avails*
> *Save that which is in thee.*

Spurgeon contrasted, on the one hand, the sanctification or consecration (in shadow) of the Levites and the priests under the old covenant, with, on the other hand, the reality of the sanctification or consecration of believers in Christ. In the new covenant, under Christ, in Christ, every believer is positionally sanctified, and from the moment of his conversion should be assured,[18] and so begin to live a life of progressive sanctification:

> You and I are not typically, but truly and really, his people. Through Jesus Christ's offering of himself once and for all, we are really set apart to be the LORD's people henceforth and forever and he says of us – I mean, of course, not of us all, but of as many as have believed in Jesus and to whom the Holy Spirit has revealed his finished work – 'I will be their God and they shall be my people'. You, believers, are sanctified in this

---

[18] See my *Assurance*.

sense, that you are now the set-apart ones unto God and you belong wholly to him. Will you think that over? 'I am now not my own. I do not belong now to the common order of men, as all the rest of men do. I am set apart. I am called out. I am taken aside. I am one of the LORD's own. I am his treasure and his portion. He has through Jesus Christ's death made me one of those of whom he says: 'They shall dwell alone, they shall not be numbered among the people'. I want you to feel it so that you may live under the power of that fact, that you may feel: 'My Lord has cleansed me. My Lord has made expiation for me. My Lord has reconciled me unto God and I am God's man, I am God's woman. I cannot live as others do. I cannot be one among you. I must come out. I must be separate. I cannot find my pleasure where you find yours. I cannot find my treasure where you find yours. I am God's, and God is mine. That wondrous transaction on the cross of which our minister has tried to speak, but of which he could not speak as he ought – that wondrous unspeakable deed upon the cross – that wonderful life and death of Jesus, has made me one of God's people, set apart unto him and as such I must live'.

When you realise that you are God's people, the next thing is to reflect that God, in sanctifying a people set them apart for his service, he made them fit for his service. You, beloved, through Christ's one great offering of his body for you, are permitted now to be the servants of God... In fact, he bought for us a sanctification which has made us the LORD's people and has enabled us to engage in his service. Do we not rejoice in this?

Next to that we have this privilege that what we do can now be accepted. Because Jesus Christ, by the offering of his body once has perfected the Father's will and has sanctified us, therefore what we do is now accepted with God...

And now we are privileged to the highest degree, being sanctified – that is to say, made into God's people, God's servants, and God's accepted servants. Every privilege which we could have had, if we had never sinned, is now ours and we are in him as his children...

'Trust in the LORD and do good; so shall you dwell in the land and certainly you shall be fed', till he comes to catch you away where you shall see what Jesus did for you when he made his body once for all a sacrifice that he might fulfil the will of the eternal Father and sanctify you and all his people unto God forever and ever. May the best of blessings rest upon all who are in Christ Jesus. Amen.

But I have omitted a vital portion from Spurgeon's sermon, because I wish to close with it. Spurgeon, in his usual pithy way, here states what I have been trying to say:

> We will not enter at this time into a detailed account of our Lord's active and passive obedience by which he magnified the law and set apart his people. I pray you, however, never fall into the error of dividing the work of Christ as some do and saying: 'Here he made atonement for sin and there he did not'. In these modern times, certain brethren have invented refinements of statement of so trivial a character that they are not even worth the trouble of thinking over and yet, like babes with a new rattle, they make a noise with them all day long. It is amusing how these wise professors make grave points out of mere hair-splitting distinctions and if we do not agree with them they give themselves mighty airs, pitying our ignorance, and esteeming themselves as superior persons who have an insight into things which ordinary Christians cannot see. God save us from having eyes which are so sharp that we are able to spy out new occasions for difference and fresh reasons for making men offenders for mere words. I believe in the life of Christ as well as in his death, and I believe that he stood for me before God as much when he walked the acres of Palestine as when he hung on the cross at Jerusalem. You cannot divide and split him in sunder and say: 'He is so far an example and so far an atonement', but you must take the entire Christ and look at him from the very first as the Lamb of God which takes away the sin of the world. 'Oh, but', they say, 'he made no atonement except in his death', which is, let me tell you, an absurdity in language. Listen a minute. When does a man die? I cannot tell you. There is the minute in which the soul separates from the body, but all the time that a man may be described as dying he is alive, is he not? A man does not suffer when actually dead. What we call the pangs of death are truly and accurately pangs of life. Death does not suffer – it is the end of suffering. A man is in life while he suffers and if they say: 'It is Christ's death that makes an atonement and not his life', I reply that death, alone and by itself, makes no atonement. Death in its natural sense and not in this modern non-natural severance from life, does make atonement – but it cannot be viewed apart from life by any unsophisticated mind. If they must have

distinctions, we could make distinctions enough to worry them of such an unprofitable business, but we have nobler work to do. To us our Lord's death seems to be the consummation of his life, the finishing stroke of a work which his Father had given him to do among the sons of men. We view him as having come in a body prepared for him to do the will of God once – and that 'once' lasted throughout his one life on earth. We will not, however, dwell on any moot point, but unfeignedly rejoice that whatever was wanted to make God's people wholly sanctified unto God, Christ has worked out. 'By the which will we are sanctified through the offering of the body of Jesus Christ once'. It is finished. Does the divine law require for our acceptance perfect submission to the will of the LORD? He has rendered it. Does it ask complete obedience to its precepts? He has presented the same. Does the fulfilled will of the LORD call for abject suffering, a sweat of blood, pangs unknown, and death, itself? Christ has presented it all, whatever that 'all' may be. As when God created, his word effected all his will, so when God redeemed, his blessed and incarnate Word has done all his will. In every point, as God looked on each day's work and said: 'It is good', so, as he looks upon each part of the work of his dear Son, he can say of it: 'It is good'. The Father joins in the verdict of his Son that it is finished – all the will of God for the sanctification of his people is accomplished.[19]

I have not quoted C.H.Spurgeon to prove my point, of course, but I am heartily glad to have his support.

---

[19] Spurgeon sermon 1527.

Made in the USA
Las Vegas, NV
21 November 2022

59976870R00056